Burning Bush

BEING A TREATISE ON THE ECSTATIC CONTEMPLATION OF THE BLESSED TRINITY

> Partial Contents: God in Himself; First Idea of God; God's Description of Himself; How to Proceed in this Contemplation; Mystery of the Father; The Word, the Second Person of the Blessed Trinity; Only Begotten Son; How St. John came by the Expression the Word; Wonders of the Third Person; Blessed Three in One; God in His Works; World of Matter from Stars to Matter; Romance of Our Little Earth; Divine View Point; God in the Heart of the Mystic.

Dom Savinien Louismet

ISBN 1-56459-566-8

Kessinger Publishing's Rare Mystical Reprints

THOUSANDS OF SCARCE BOOKS ON THESE AND OTHER SUBJECTS:

Freemasonry * Akashic * Alchemy * Alternative Health * Ancient Civilizations * Anthroposophy * Astrology * Astronomy * Aura * Bible Study * Cabalah * Cartomancy * Chakras * Clairvoyance * Comparative Religions * Divination * Druids * Eastern Thought * Egyptology * Esoterism * Essenes * Etheric * ESP * Gnosticism * Great White Brotherhood * Hermetics * Kabalah * Karma * Knights Templar * Kundalini * Magic * Meditation * Mediumship * Mesmerism * Metaphysics * Mithraism * Mystery Schools * Mysticism * Mythology * Numerology * Occultism * Palmistry * Pantheism * Parapsychology * Philosophy * Prosperity * Psychokinesis * Psychology * Pyramids * Qabalah * Reincarnation * Rosicrucian * Sacred Geometry * Secret Rituals * Secret Societies * Spiritism * Symbolism * Tarot * Telepathy * Theosophy * Transcendentalism * Upanishads * Vedanta * Wisdom * Yoga * *Plus Much More!*

DOWNLOAD A FREE CATALOG AT:
www.kessinger.net

OR EMAIL US AT:
books@kessinger.net

THE BURNING BUSH

GLADNESS IN THE MORNING
(CH. XXXI)

PREFACE

SUMMARY.—Why the contemplation of the Most Holy Trinity is here called ecstatical. That ecstasy may be either active or passive. The purpose of the present treatise. Its division.

IN order not to begin this new treatise—the seventh in the series of my books on mysticism—with a misunderstanding, we must first of all state in what sense the contemplation of the Most Holy Trinity is here called ecstatical.

There are two sorts of ecstasies, an active one and a purely passive one. Passive ecstasy is that which is caused by the intensity of the supernatural impressions which a fervent soul receives at times: it is only of this sort of ecstasy that most spiritual writers speak. Yet there is also another kind which might well be called the *active one;* it is that which consists in a spontaneous movement of the soul, in its endeavour to quit self and all created things, in order to apply herself to God alone. It is in this latter sense that we speak here of ecstatical contemplation.

The contemplation of the Most Holy Trinity must perforce be ecstatical first of all in that manner; only later may the fervent soul hope to experience the purely passive ecstasy if God be pleased to grant it. However, we do not at present take this eventuality into consideration.

The purpose of this new treatise is not to restate, after so many others, the metaphysical proof of God, or scientifically to expound His infinite perfections. My ordinary readers have no need of such a demonstration. More modest—some perhaps would say, more exalted—is my ambition. I simply aim at leading them up to the contemplation of God in whom they already believe with their whole heart; so that they may find their joy in Him, that they may learn how to play with Him *as most dear children* (Eph. v, 1) the beautiful game of reciprocal love, that they may break out into praise of His Divine Goodness and Majesty.

It were therefore a mistake to seek in the following pages anything else but what I have intended to present to my readers—namely, a practical introduction to the

PREFACE

art of dealing lovingly with God in the secret of one's own heart. I am following up the general plan outlined in chapters v and vi of my second volume (*The Mystical Life*). We are still, as in volumes iv, v, and vi, busy about the first function of the mystical life, which is Divine contemplation; we are now to treat of its supreme object—namely, the Most Holy Trinity.

Already in a previous volume we have had occasion to speak at some length of the respective activities, so to say, of each of the three Divine Persons in regard to the mystic (*cf. The Mystical Life*, chs. viii, ix, x, xv, xvi). In the present work we place ourselves at a different point of view—namely, that of the contemplative activity of the fervent Christian himself in regard to the great mystery.

Throughout all this treatise the reader will do well to remember what has been said in chapter xx of *The Mystical Life*, as to each man being supremely alone with God alone. In the light of this principle many of the following pages, which might otherwise remain unintelligible, will be, we trust, quite clear.

With his whole heart and soul, with his whole being, ought the contemplative to approach the Mystery of the Divine Essence, and he must be ready to pay the price of so noble an objective: to strain his every power of soul and body in a mighty, long-sustained, and yet at the same time very pleasing effort, bearing successively upon diverse points of the vast field of knowledge.

This is, perhaps, the most halting and uncouth of all the books I have thus far written, though it is the one which made the greatest demand upon my energies and the one which I wrote with greatest enthusiasm and care and fervour of love.

No wonder it should seem incoherent and its chapters a succession of abortive attempts —no wonder, indeed, when we take into consideration the sublimity of the subject and the vileness of the writer. All I can say in excuse of my rashness in attempting such a high theme is that I had to do it under penalty of leaving my series of treatises incomplete. May the good and

PREFACE

loving God forgive me and help my readers! It is in His power to make even such a wretched instrument as this book of mine, the means of drawing them nearer to Him. At least, amidst all its shortcomings, it has one redeeming feature—namely, this, that as in my book on *The Mystery of Jesus*, in this one also I have drawn largely from the fountains of living waters of the Holy Scriptures, and copiously poured them out all over the surface of my little garden; so that even so barren a plot of ground may yet be found to flourish and exhale a sweet odour and bear some fruit unto eternal life both for my dear readers and for me.

The treatise is divided into three books, thus:

>   Book I.—God in Himself.
>   Book II.—God in His Works.
>   Book III.—God in the Heart of the Mystic.

This may not be the order that would recommend itself to certain minds. Perhaps some would prefer that we should begin in a first book with the testimony of God in our heart, then proceed in a second book to read the glorious Name of God written in flaming letters all over the magnificent scroll of the universe; and finally rise to the consideration of God in Himself, in the ineffable Trinity of His Persons. Such would indeed be the logical order to follow, were we bent upon writing a theoretical or academic treatise on God. But quite different is our purpose.

We take the fact of the existence of God and that of the revelation of the Trinity of His Persons as granted. At the very outset, we fasten our gaze exclusively upon God in Himself, in the unity and unicity of His Divine Essence splendidly blooming out into the Trinity of His Persons; and we would even wish, were this possible, to do nothing else but lovingly to contemplate him thus. But, as we are as yet but pilgrims on earth, we soon grow tired of this sublime exercise and have perforce to turn to a less exhausting process, that of contemplating the same Triune God in the mirror of the works of His Hands at large and, at last, more particularly in His dim but so sweet revelation of Himself in our own heart.

CONTENTS

PART I—GOD IN HIMSELF

PAGES

PREFACE vii

CHAPTER I.—WHAT THE ANCHORITE SAID . 1—8
That the Priest is a Master in Israel, who meets God in an official capacity, and also if he wishes, unofficially, in the secret of his own heart. What may be wrong in the method of mental prayer, and how it can be set right. An attempt to do so and what followed upon it. That the heart is the real master of the spiritual craft, and love the finest of fine arts.

CHAPTER II.—A FIRST IDEA OF GOD WITH WHICH TO BEGIN . . . . 9—13
That God is the most real, simple, entrancing being. We cannot grasp the extent of the wonder He is. How man on earth views the Divine Loveliness. Have we succeeded in our attempt at forming an idea of God?

CHAPTER III.—GOD'S DESCRIPTION OF HIMSELF 14—19
Moses and the burning bush. The burning bush of Creation. One only God in three Persons. We must never separate these two ideas: God and Trinity, but read them one into the other. By these words *I am who am*, God reveals to us the infinite intensity of His own inner life. An apt reply to infidel philosophers.

THE BURNING BUSH

CHAPTER IV.—HOW TO PROCEED IN THIS CONTEMPLATION . . . . . 20—25

The process devised by some in order to arrive at union with God. Neither the Church nor the Scriptures teach the method of abstraction. The child's notion of God is the right one, to which philosophers and theologians finally return. The way we recommend.

CHAPTER V.—WHEN, WHERE, AND HOW TO DO IT? . . . . . 26—31

Two distinct answers to be given to this set of questions. The first is: Whenever, Wheresoever, and Howsoever one feels inclined. That the spirit of prayer is free. Examples as to the special worship of each of the three Divine Persons. Some beautiful practices in regard to the Holy Spirit.

CHAPTER VI.—ANOTHER ANSWER TO THE SAME QUESTIONS . . . . 32—38

We are to pay especial attention to God the Father at Mass. Why. Also before natural scenery by day or night. To God the Son, when out of Mass we visit the Blessed Sacrament, the eyes of faith discerning Him under the Sacred Species. To the Holy Ghost, when at private prayer, and all through the day's various occupations.

CHAPTER VII.—IN WHAT SPIRIT THIS IS TO BE DONE . . . . . 39—45

The reason why many have erred about the Blessed Trinity. Our purpose not to make theologians. No irreverent curiosity, but simple faith and love. The Church has carefully set down, in her sacred liturgy, the

CONTENTS

terms in which we are to think and speak of the Blessed Trinity. The Nicene Creed, and the Preface of the Mass of the Blessed Trinity.

CHAPTER VIII.—THE MYSTERY OF THE FATHER   46—50

The mystery of the Divine life. That the Divine Operations give rise to the Trinity of Persons. Despair of the man who would express God and love Him adequately. What man cannot do God does. Saying that God is the Creator gives no idea of what He is in Himself.

CHAPTER IX.—MORE ABOUT GOD THE FATHER   51—57

How this should be understood. That whatever is said of the other two Persons and of the Divine nature makes us know more of the Father. The Collects of the Mass. Sayings of Our Lord in the Gospel. How a devotional treatise might be made on this entrancing subject.

CHAPTER X.—THE WORD, THE SECOND PERSON OF THE BLESSED TRINITY - - -   58—65

A new appellation of the second Person, peculiar to St. John. Silence of the other writers of the New Testament in regard to the Word, whilst this appellation is found with the identical meaning of St. John in several passages of the Old Testament. It does not appear that the inspired writers, still less the People of God of that time, understood its full import.

CHAPTER XI.—THE ONLY-BEGOTTEN SON   66—78

That the second Person proceeds from the first by way of generation. Testimony of the Father, of the Son, of the Holy Spirit.

THE BURNING BUSH

PAGES

CHAPTER XII.—HOW ST. JOHN CAME BY THE EXPRESSION "THE WORD" · · 79—85

He did not borrow it from Greek lore, but it was revealed to him straight from heaven. Sublimity of the first verses of his Gospel. The *Logos* of Hellenic literature is but an abstraction, that of St. John and of the Old Testament a living and Divine Person. Striking corollary.

CHAPTER XIII.—THE WONDERS OF THE THIRD PERSON · · · · · 86—96

The Holy Ghost was known as a Divine Person, by Mary and Joseph, though not by the People of God in the Old Testament. Danger of our conceiving the Holy Ghost as inferior to the Father and the Son. Precisions formulated in the Nicene Creed. Personal characteristics of the Holy Ghost: the substantial Sweetness of the Divine Essence. Testimony of Our Lord. Fecundity of the Holy Ghost, and how we stand in His regard.

CHAPTER XIV.—THE BLESSED THREE IN ONE 97—106

A felicitous dogmatic formula. How the three Divine Persons are supremely One. Various images. A mystery it will remain for ever. Unicity of the Divine Essence and three diverse ways of possessing it. In each Person the mystery stands revealed. *Actus Purus* three times over.

PART II—GOD IN HIS WORKS.

CHAPTER XV.—ON THE OPERATIONS OF GOD CALLED "AD EXTRA" · · · · 109—112

What is meant and also what is not meant by "operations *ad extra*." How numerous and

CONTENTS

varied. All summed up in the three: Creation, Redemption, Sanctification—appropriated respectively to the Father, the Son, and the Holy Ghost—and further summed up in the supreme one of *the fulfilling of Jesus Christ*.

CHAPTER XVI.—ON THE PRETENDED PLURALITY OF WORLDS . . . . . 113—118

Two attitudes possible in front of the universe. No scientific evidence in favour of the hypothesis of a plurality of independent closed systems of stars, or of planets being inhabited by other human races. Dogmatic Revelation dead against the last supposition. We have a better plurality of worlds to consider.

CHAPTER XVII.—THE GREATEST WORLD UNDER THE BLESSED TRINITY . . . 119—126

The Human Soul of Our Lord Jesus Christ. Infinitude of grace and power it derives from the hypostatic union. Divine Diffusiveness. The Divine Plan. Order of the Divine Emanations.

CHAPTER XVIII.—THE NEXT GREATEST WORLD, THE BLESSED VIRGIN MARY . . 127—133

She is the only created World after Jesus, in which God has not suffered disappointment. The great things God has done to her. How *full of grace*. A revelation of God's loving-kindness and mercy. The universal Mother. The pedestal of the Golden Candlestick.

CHAPTER XIX.—THE THIRD GREATEST WORLD 134—142

The Church of the Predestinate. Of what elements it is made up. God has suffered some disappointment first in angels, then in the human race. Each predestinate, a little world. Each single angel, a whole nature.

The first Church Militant. That God reveals Himself in the Saints. Their wonderful personality. Vessels of gold, adorned with precious stones. Their various orders.

CHAPTER XX.—THE WORLD OF MATTER, FROM STARS TO ATOMS · · · · 143—151

The humblest of worlds, and still very stupendous. The untutored Arab *versus* the European atheist. A starlit night. The atom of hydrogen. The composition of matter—of ether. Man's mind superior to the world of matter. Creation a veil on the radiant face of God.

CHAPTER XXI.—THE ROMANCE OF OUR LITTLE EARTH · · · · 152—159

The Earth in itself an object full of interest. The abode of Godlike man, of the Militant Church, of the Blessed Sacrament. Narrow limits within which man can exercise his sovereignty. That the Mystic has chosen *the better part*.

CHAPTER XXII.—A FALLEN WORLD IN COURSE OF BEING RECLAIMED · · · · 160—167

The human race. How God deals with it. Every man a little world. Worth and capacity of a human soul. Actual population of the globe. Rate of births and deaths. How this works out thus far, for a grand total. Our own image in God. Original sin no obstacle to the plan of God.

CHAPTER XXIII.—THE TERRIBLE WORLD OF REPROBATION · · · · 168—177

Is God made manifest therein? Spoiled materials forming a hideous chaos. Hell it-

CONTENTS

self a real world and the work of the Blessed Trinity. The case of the reprobate. God a torment to him. He does not wish to cease to be. Monuments of the Divine Justice.

CHAPTER XXIV.—THE DIVINE VIEW-POINT - 178—184
God always right. The virus of original sin and the grace of Redemption. Various oppositions. The alternative. In the hands of our free will. How sin itself turns to the glory of God.

CHAPTER XXV.—THE DIVINE SOLITARINESS IN THE MIDST OF CREATION - - - 185—198
Immanence and Transcendence—two aspects of a Divine fact. That God is ever creating—intimately present in every parcel of the universe. The six days of Genesis and natural laws. God our centre. Full import of the term transcendence. Theologians and mystical writers on this subject. Fundamental nothingness of all "that is not God." That God is His own all-sufficing company in the Trinity of His Persons.

PART III—GOD IN THE HEART OF THE MYSTIC

CHAPTER XXVI.—INTRODUCTORY TO THIS THIRD PART - - - - - 201—204
That one does not know God until one has viewed Him under this aspect. That this treatise would not be complete without such a presentment of God. Inspired writers and saintly authors have opened the way. A prejudice which ought to be broken down.

THE BURNING BUSH

PAGES

CHAPTER XXVII.—THE MARVELLOUS ADVENTURE . . . . . 205—207
Few seek after God. How thrilling an adventure as compared to all others. Its wide range. It captivates the whole man. What it reveals to him.

CHAPTER XXVIII.—WHAT HAPPENS THEN . 208—210
When an earthly lover meets his beloved. With the Mystic in search of God the process is reversed. Beginning of the little love-drama.

CHAPTER XXIX.—THE ENCOUNTER . . 211—214
What takes place in the secret of the soul. Transports of joy and illusions. Darkness and Desolation. What to do then. Gold in the crucible.

CHAPTER XXX.— A CHALLENGE . . 215—220
The key to the lives of the Saints. The Soul's reply. The Roman Coliseum. Another Coliseum. The spectators. The spectacle. The Lord as *a warrior*. What dost thou say?

CHAPTER XXXI.—GLADNESS IN THE MORNING 221—224
Weeping in the evening and its remedy. A vision in a Dream. The three Divine Persons and a Little Boy. A question. The reply. Waking up and after.

CHAPTER XXXII.—THE GOLDEN PYRAMID . 225—230
Gird up thy loins. What for. The Knight in the Palace of Quiet. What he wishes to see. Enigmatic representation of the Blessed Trinity. Petition of Knight Fidelis.

CONTENTS

Chapter XXXIII.—The Supremest Experience . . . . . 231—237

The living Crucifix. Through Him into the Golden Pyramid. What then. How long. Limitations of the transforming Union. Feelings of the Soul about it. Back into the Palace of Quiet. The Soul enlarged and what it sighs after. St. Thomas Aquinas. Knight Fidelis will die of his wound.

Epilogue. . . . . 238—240

PART I—GOD IN HIMSELF

THE BURNING BUSH

CHAPTER I

What the Anchorite Said

SUMMARY.—The priest a *Magister in Israel* in the art of communing with God. Meeting God officially. Also unofficially, in the secret of one's heart. Something wrong in his method of mental prayer. How to set about it. Tell God what is uppermost in your heart. What followed upon the attempt. Praise of the heart over the mind: it is the real master of the spiritual life. The finest of fine arts.

A PRIEST well-known for his zeal and piety comes one day to an old anchorite, and, without any preamble, humbly proffers his request:

"Please, Father, do teach me the art of communing with God."

"What," replied the old anchorite, "is it for me to give you lessons in that art? Are you not a *Magister in Israel?* With your daily Mass and Divine Office you are constantly, one might almost say day and night, in touch with the Divine Majesty, communing with God, treating with Him of the affairs of the world."

THE PRIEST. "True. But that is my official meeting with God, in the name of the Church and of the whole Christian people, and what I have to say is, to use a familiar expression, cut and dried and set down for me. I try, indeed, to discharge this duty faithfully and devoutly, but I wish moreover to do something else; to commune with God unofficially, in the secret of my own heart, sweetly and familiarly and spontaneously, after the manner described in certain recent books; or, to be perhaps a little more precise, after the manner set down in the Introit of to-day's Mass. (This happened to be the Tuesday of the second week of Lent.) The Introit is taken from Ps. xxvi, 8 and is as follows: '*My heart hath spoken to Thee; my face hath sought Thee; Thy face, O Lord, will I seek.*'"

THE ANCHORITE. "What about daily mental prayer? Are you faithful to it?"

THE PRIEST. "Yes; but that is precisely where the trouble comes in. I make

WHAT THE ANCHORITE SAID

it a practice every evening carefully to prepare the points of the morrow's meditation. Then in the morning, I consider these points as attentively as I can, but when it comes to producing affections, somehow I find it impossible to press anything out of my heart, and I have an impression that something is wrong in my method, though I could not tell what it is."

"I see," said THE ANCHORITE thoughtfully. "I see. Well, the remedy is not far to seek.

"Suppose now, that instead of meeting God first with your mind and only afterwards with your heart, you reverse the process, and begin by pressing your heart into service; it will make all the difference in the world."

THE PRIEST (*eagerly*). "Will it indeed? How good! Now, please tell me how to set about it? What shall I say to God to begin with?"

THE ANCHORITE. "My friend, do you mean that I should dictate to you your first words? This were too ridiculous. Simply tell the loving God who is here, and is intently listening to you, whatever is uppermost in your heart. Speak! I am not going to say another word until you have done it."

After a few seconds of embarrassed silence the good priest, raising his eyes upwards and, perhaps, unconsciously joining his hands, slowly and deliberately spoke these words in an undertone:

"My God! Thou art my God. I confess Thou art the sovereign Lord of all and my very own loving Father. To Thee I am indebted for all I have and am, but it seems to me as though I had never yet returned Thee thanks for all this.

"Thanks, then, O my God! hearty thanks to Thine Infinite Goodness. Oh! how good Thou art! how sweet! how lovely! and how beautiful must Thou be! Oh! when shall I see Thy countenance? Then shall I be happy. *Satiabor cum apparuerit gloria tua. . . .*" (Ps. xvi, 15).

Which having said, or rather sighed out, the dear man coloured up deeply and his face became radiant.

In the meanwhile the anchorite had been taking down in shorthand that effusion as it was artlessly poured out of the fervid

WHAT THE ANCHORITE SAID

heart. He now translated the cryptic signs into ordinary writing and showed them to the good priest, who was simply amazed at what he had been saying, and stammered out: *Eructavit cor meum verbum bonum* (Ps. xliv, 2), "Verily, my heart hath uttered a good word."

THE ANCHORITE. "Yes; that is just it, my friend. Well, now you see, you had it in yourself to begin communing with God, speaking to Him heart to heart. You have done it; you have made a beginning; what remains now for you to do is simply to carry on. Try and discover your own feelings when you advert to the presence of God who is always at hand, then express them in as direct, simple and candid a way as you possibly can. Allow your heart to have its say. Let flow freely the tender filial feelings which press upwards towards Him who so prodigiously loves you, and who, independently of your personal debt of gratitude to Him, so richly deserves to be loved for His own sake. That is the way to commune with God."

After a pause THE ANCHORITE continued:

"In the beginning this novel exercise may seem somewhat awkward: it does not seem natural thus to hearken to the promptings of one's own heart in preference to the thoughts of one's mind. But this is a wrong impression due mainly to the fact of our having been spoiled by too bookish an education. If you persevere you will soon grow so used to it that it will become as a second nature, and this will make you very happy. The heart takes much for granted. It suppresses a great deal of the slow plodding of the mind. It has wings, the wings of a carrier pigeon, and flies straight as an arrow, home to its love.

"Moreover, it is a fact that the mind is curious, inclined to pride, easily puffed up, secretly self-seeking, unbending and harsh, whilst the heart, under pressure of Divine grace, is the real master of the spiritual life.

"Are you surprised to hear me say that the heart, not the brain, is the real master of the spiritual life? Yes, the heart is, under God, the prime mover in the business of communing with God—the heart, not the intellect. The heart is tender, disinterested, indefatigable; a revealer and an initiator, both charming and captivating. Yes, charmed, indeed, and captivated by his own heart will a Christian be, if he only knows how to make it speak and will hearken to what it tells. But this is a small thing: why, the Christian heart even charms and captivates God Himself. God cares not at all for the discourses of your mind, whilst He does lovingly incline His ear to catch the faintest sounds of love and praise which proceed from the true Christian heart. Only a moment ago, your heart produced the first little syllables of love, and you were entranced at the sweetness of the melody. Now, when it is so good only to begin, what will it be to go on, to unravel the melody as it will sing itself out? How sweet to pour it all out in the ears of the good and loving God, thus communing with Him not with your brains, but with your affections.

"Is not this the finest of fine arts? Little by little you will become proficient in it.

"But what am I saying—little by little?

THE BURNING BUSH

Promptly, impetuously, will the Holy Spirit lift your soul above itself, above your ordinary purely human practice of faith and hope, lift you up on the wings of Understanding and Wisdom—those two sublimest gifts—causing you to travel in an instant an infinite space, to find your rest in the very bosom of God."

So spake THE ANCHORITE.

CHAPTER II

A First Idea of God with which to Begin

SUMMARY.—The most real, simple, entrancing being. We cannot grasp the extent of the wonder. How man on earth views the loveliness of God. Effusions. Have we succeeded in our attempt at forming an idea of God?

GOD! God! Oh, what is God?
We know—at least in theory, even if we do not let it influence us in the practice of our life—we know that God is the most real, noble, beautiful, magnificent, and majestic being, and at the same time the most simple, familiar, affable; the nearest to each one of us, the most inclined towards us; the most communicative, sweet, charming, alluring, entrancing; the most loving, tender, and affectionate: infinitely above everything else that is so, in the realm of nature, or of grace, or of glory.

Let us suppose that all the rays of beauty and of goodness which are scattered in this visible universe and in the world of souls

THE BURNING BUSH

and of pure spirits could be united and, so to say, fused into one single created being, and that the beauty and goodness of this one single being could be intensified one hundred millionfold, and this again multiplied by one hundred million, we should have what we could consider as an object of very dazzling splendour indeed; and yet, compared with the Divine loveliness, the beauty and goodness of that extraordinary being would be less than a drop of water compared with the ocean. Do we need to demonstrate this? Is it not self-evident? God is the Absolute, the Infinite, the *I am who am* (Exod. iii, 14), whilst all that exists outside Him is but a shadow of being. Multiply a shadow as many million times as you will, it but remains what it is, a pure shadow, unworthy to enter into parallel with the substance which casts it. Our Lord one day told St. Catherine of Siena: "I am who am and thou art who is not."

God in His own sweet Self is a shoreless and bottomless ocean of life and light and sanctity.

Do we understand this, O my soul?

A FIRST IDEA OF GOD

Of course not: or rather let us say that we perfectly understand that it must be so, but we cannot grasp the extent of the wonder.

O my Lord God, most Holy; Thou the One, the Strong, the absolutely Good, the All-lovely; help Thy poor servant somehow to represent to himself and to picture to his brethren a glimpse of the ineffable splendour of Thy Divine Essence, of the sweetness of Thy sanctity, of the gracious condescension of Thy sovereign heart, which wants to be loved of me, even of me, of little me!

Suppose a man had never been able to look up to the sun because of some cruel infirmity which held him bent double, but that he could see the image of the sun reflected in a tiny dewdrop at the top of a blade of grass. Could such a man flatter himself that he possessed a just idea of the splendour of the sun? Now that represents very nearly the situation of those on earth in regard to God. They view the loveliness of God, not in itself, but only as it is reflected in that dewdrop of the material universe: "*Ecce gentes quasi stilla situlae,*" says the prophet (Isa. xl, 15). *Behold the Gentiles are as a drop of a bucket,* which has been dipped in the fountain.

O splendour of God, which to me seems so refulgent already when only seen through the tiny glass of our universe, can it be that I am destined soon, steadily and fearlessly to gaze upon the luminous orb of Thy Divine Essence, even as the eagle looks fixedly at the sun? Thou art my Sun, and on the day of the Beatific Vision, Thou wilt grant me to see Thee face to face without being consumed or dazzled into blindness.

Meanwhile, it is Thy sovereign pleasure that I should contemplate Thee alternately, first in the marvels of this visible world, which is the work of Thy hands, and then, as often as I may, in the Dark Cloud, that is to say, in Thy very Self without the interposition of any created image, by the exercise of faith and ardent love, whenever Thou vouchsafest to help Thy poor servant by special grace. And whilst I am as yet unable to see Thee unveiled, this at least is granted me, to feel the warm rays of Thy

A FIRST IDEA OF GOD

Divine Goodness enveloping me on every side.

O my God and my all, I do desire thus to contemplate Thee during the remaining years of my pilgrimage here below, to spend the rest of my life seeking after Thee, striving to lay hold of Thee, humbly making love to Thee and enjoying Thee as much as Thou wilt be pleased to grant me.

My soul, what have we done? We have tried to express God, to give some idea of Him; have we succeeded? We have been stammering only.

Whatever we can say of God (and precisely because we can say it) is unworthy of Him. Would even angelic speech, that of the cherub or seraph, be equal to the task of telling us what God is? No! This is His glory, that alone His own Divine Word, an infinite Person, expresses Him worthily.

Let us hold our peace and adore.

CHAPTER III

GOD'S DESCRIPTION OF HIMSELF

SUMMARY.—The vision of the Burning Bush. God speaks to us also from the burning bush of Creation. The one only God in three Persons. Never separate these two ideas, God and Trinity; read them one into the other. "I am who am" tells the infinite intensity of God's inner life. The reply to infidel philosophers. Effusion of admiration and love.

"*Now Moses fed the sheep of Jethro, his father-in-law, the priest of Madian: and he drove the flock to the inner part of the desert, and came to the mountain of God, Horeb. And the Lord appeared to him in a flame of fire out of the midst of a bush, and he saw that the bush was on fire and was not burnt. And Moses said: I will go and see this great sight, why the bush is not burnt. And when the Lord saw that he went forward to see, He called to him out of the midst of the bush, and said: Moses, Moses. And he answered: Here I am. And He said: Come not nigh hither, put off the shoes*

GOD'S DESCRIPTION OF HIMSELF

from thy feet, for the place whereon thou standest is holy ground. And He said: I am the God of your fathers, the God of Abraham, the God of Isaac, and the God of Jacob. I am who am" (Exod. iii, 1-6 and 14).

The Lord God speaks to every soul of good will from the burning bush of creation. Here by the word creation we must understand not only this material universe, but at the same time the world of grace and that of glory—a bush that is ever burning and never consumed. Now what does the Lord God tell us? First of all He warns us how we ought to stand on the holy ground of Divine ecstatic contemplation—with what purity of intention, detachment from all things created, and feelings of reverent awe and love. All this is inculcated in the words: "Put off the shoes from thy feet."

Then the Lord God goes on to reveal Himself to the mystic, as the one only God in three Divine Persons: "I am the God of Abraham, the God of Isaac, the God of Jacob. I am who am." And just as Moses, prostrate on the ground, hid his face and durst not look at God, though he heard Him and spoke to Him, so also the contemplative, prostrate on his own nothingness dares not look at the Divine Essence, nay cannot do so, but he nevertheless hears what God tells him of His own Divine Self, and is filled with joy at this wonderful revelation.

God is the Blessed Trinity of the Father, the Son, and the Holy Ghost. We must never separate, nay we must be careful ever to keep joined together in our mind these two ideas, God and the Trinity: we must see these two ideas one into the other. There is no other God than the Blessed Trinity of the Father, the Son, and the Holy Ghost. The Trinity of Persons is not something secondary in God, superadded from outside to the Divine Essence; the Trinity is God, the three Divine Persons are the one only God. God is essentially these three distinct Persons, the Father, the Son, and the Holy Ghost. To be God is to be the Father, the Son, and the Holy Ghost.

When God tells us magnificently *I am who am* (Exod. iii, 14), He reveals to us the infinite intensity of His Divine Life. True, when we glance into the abyss of light which this definition of God by Himself gives, our purblind intellect cannot as yet, without Divine assistance, discern therein the Trinity of Persons. But this Divine assistance has been granted to us. We have been told distinctly, in many scriptural passages, that God has a Son; and in the fulness of time this Son of God was made man and lived among men and was seen by them *full of grace and truth* (John i, 14), and has left shining and imperishable monuments of His passage here upon earth. It has also been revealed to us that there is in God yet another mode of production and procession, distinct from that of generation, and that it results in a third Person, the Holy Spirit. Thus are we made to understand all that is implied in this declaration *I am who am.* We realize that God is a Trinity of Persons and that whenever we name God, we name the Blessed Trinity, we must think of the Blessed Trinity, we must believe in and confess and adore the Most Holy Trinity of the Father, the Son, and the Holy Spirit.

THE BURNING BUSH

O my God, with what joy do I render to Thee this homage! I believe in Thee, O Most Holy Trinity; to Thee do I submit my feeble understanding; gladly do I embrace this revelation of Thyself by Thyself to us under the veil of faith, pending the time not so very far distant, when, as I firmly hope from Thine ineffable Goodness, I shall receive the fulness of Thy revelation in the splendours of the Beatific Vision.

Infidel philosophers would like to reduce Thee, O my God, to a mere abstract idea, a vain word without meaning, a vague and impersonal thing: and behold, Thou revealest Thyself as being not only personal as we see that we ourselves are, but thrice Personal. Thou, O Lord God, subsistest in three distinct hypostases: so opulent, so magnificent is Thy being! Thou art more personal than we can possibly conceive or realize. This fact has to be revealed to us, and even when thus revealed, we can as yet take hold of it but by faith. But, O my God, how sweet it is for us to know that Thou vouchsafest to draw near each one of us, with Thy whole Divine Self, with Thy three Divine Persons.

GOD'S DESCRIPTION OF HIMSELF

In vain does the poor sinner, in his blindness, draw back and withdraw himself from Thee, turn his back on Thee, enjoying Thy benefactions and denying that they come from Thee, O Most Holy Trinity. It remains true, nevertheless, that our dealings with Thee, O my God, must, on our own part, be personal, most intimate and loving, whilst Thine own dealings with each one of us are three times personal, because Thou art one God in three distinct Persons, the Father, the Son, and the Holy Ghost.

To Thee be glory for ever.

CHAPTER IV

How to Proceed in this Contemplation

SUMMARY.—The process devised by some in order to arrive at a pure concept of the Divine Essence. The Church does not teach the method of abstraction nor Holy Scripture either. The child's notion of God, the right one, to which philosopher and theologian finally return. Simplicity of little children. The way we recommend: A lively method, based upon the very nature of the Divine Essence. Circumincession. The blending of notions which our contemplation of the Blessed Trinity demands, until the experience of "mystical theology" supervenes.

LEARNED and saintly personages have devised a certain process by which the soul may, with the grace of God, arrive at the pure concept of the Divine Essence. Such, among others, are first the pseudo-Areopagite, then the author of the treatise *De adhaerendo Deo*, long attributed to Blessed Albertus Magnus;

then again the anonymous author of *The Cloud of Unknowing* whom Father Baker follows in his *Sancta Sophia*.

It is not for me to find fault with them in this matter: at times I have used their books and found profit in so doing. However, we must all admit that nowhere does Holy Church teach her children the method of abstraction; far otherwise, as anyone familiar with the whole range of the sacred liturgy may convince himself. St. Augustine, though himself one of the mightiest philosophical geniuses the world ever produced, does not hesitate to call our attention to the fact that very seldom does Holy Writ bring forward or express the Divine properties in the abstract. "Quae propriè de Deo dicuntur, quaeque in nulla creatura inveniuntur, rarò ponit Scriptura divina" (*De Trinitate*, Lib. i, c. 2).

Our first concept of God is a very formless and obscure one, as of something indefinite, something, indeed, infinitely grand, and good, and beautiful, but without any distinct shape, so to say. The mind of the child, in thinking of God, cannot catch at anything: for him God is God, simply

THE BURNING BUSH

that and nothing else. When the learned Christian has gone the round of all philosophical and theological speculations about the Supreme Being, he comes back to this, the child's notion of God, and finds it to be the very best. He exclaims: "O my God, what art Thou? Thou art God and all is said, O God, my God!" The more he clings to this obscure, formless idea the nearer is he to the truth. It is in this contemplation, if ever, that we must return to the simplicity of little children, allowing ourselves to be led thereto much more by love than by understanding, confessing freely that, so far as understanding is concerned, we are unable to do aught but stammer with the prophet: *A, a, a, Domine Deus, ecce nescio loqui quia puer ego sum: Ah, ah, ah, Lord God, behold, I cannot speak, for I am but a child* (Jer. i, 6), and relinquishing the task of discoursing for that of loving and being loved, kissing and being kissed. *Let Him kiss me with the kiss of His mouth,* exclaims the little bride at the very beginning of the Canticle of Canticles.

Now, here is the way I would have you,

my dear reader, proceed in this contemplation.

Address yourself successively and separately to each of the three Divine Persons: adore that Person for His own sake, and yet be careful to adore in that Person, at the same time, each one of the other two; thus you will derive the special benefit of a distinct knowledge and love of each of the three Divine Persons, and thereby gain an increased realization of the supereminent unity of the Divine Essence. Thus you will enter deeper and deeper into the mystery of the life of God in Himself, and of our relations with each Divine Person.

I mean it in this wise.

Address yourself to the first Person of the Most Holy Trinity, the Father. Bring to remembrance all that you know which constitutes Him the very first Person as we describe it in a subsequent chapter (Ch. VIII). Praise Him for this, and then go one step further and consider that He has in Himself eternally His Divine Son and His Holy Spirit of love, and adore them in Him.

Proceed in the same manner in your

contemplation of the second Person, the Son.

First apply your mind and heart to the appreciation of what constitutes Him, the second Person, and what special excellencies shine in Him in consequence; and then, as the second step in this process of contemplation, notice that He has ever with Him His Divine Father and His Holy Ghost; adore them in Him.

Follow the same mode of contemplation in behalf of the Holy Spirit. Consider what constitutes Him, the third Person, and characterizes Him as such, and how, indeed, He is inseparable from the Father and the Son; adore Him for His own sake and adore Them in Him.

This is not an artificial method, but a lively mode of procedure based upon the very nature of the Divine Essence as revealed to us in the *deposit of faith*. One cannot long practise it without entering somewhat, even during one's pilgrim days, *into the joy of the Lord*, into the secret of His Divine operations, into light unspeakable.

The presence of the other two Persons

HOW TO PROCEED

in each separate Person is a very beautiful property of the Divine Essence, which we must never cease to admire, and reverence, and praise.

It is called *Circumincession*, but we need not mind the learned word, as long as we apprehend the Divine reality it serves to express in human language.

In this contemplation of the Blessed Trinity there must therefore be found a blending in our mind of the abstract theological notions and catechetical formulas, together with what we can of our own conjecture and express about God, from our notions of things created: until it shall please Him, of His own gracious Goodness, to vouchsafe to us the ineffable soul-experience of "mystical theology."

The Blessed Three in One, this is the refulgent Dark Cloud impenetrable, gazing upon which the soul exclaims: "O God! O my All in All! O fire of Love!" but soon, silent, motionless, she concentrates all her energy upon the act of loving.

CHAPTER V

When, Where, and How

SUMMARY.—Two distinct answers to be given to this set of questions. In this chapter we give the first answer, to this effect—namely, Whenever, Wherever, and However you feel inclined. The spirit of prayer is free. Examples as to the special worship of each of the three Divine Persons. Some beautiful practices in regard to the Holy Spirit.

DO you, O my dear reader, now ask when, where, and how to apply the principles enunciated in the preceding chapter? The reply to this query is twofold. In this chapter we give our first answer.

Adore more particularly any one of the three Divine Persons, either the Father, or the Son, or the Holy Spirit, for His own sake, whenever and wherever and howsoever you happen to feel inclined to do so. The spirit of prayer, the spirit of adoration and of fervent outpourings of love, knows no limits of time and place, no etiquette or ceremonious observance, obeys no set rules, breathes out when and where and how it listeth. No one knows beforehand when it will arise or where it will lead. No matter. The only important thing is that you should be ready to welcome it as soon as you feel its presence and that you should follow it.

Thus, at times you will be suddenly stirred with filial emotions of love and gratitude to God the Father, or feel yourself led into the entrancing contemplation of His abysmal Sanctity. At once yield to these precious feelings, give vent to them, give them voice, follow eagerly the train of thoughts and of burning affections which may arise in consequence. Follow after, follow after, panting, breathless, self-forgetting, lost to all things created. You will come out of these ecstatic moments with deeper knowledge both of God the Father and in Him of the other two Persons. Not, of course, knowledge that you could put into words, but experimental knowledge, "mystical theology" proper.

Or, is it the second Person of the Blessed Trinity, the Word, who, quite unaccountably, happens to captivate and sweetly to compel your loving attention, either as He is from all eternity in the bosom of the Father, or again in some of the delightful mysteries of His sacred Humanity?

Then, of course, contemplate Him, eagerly feed your soul with the sweets of His blessed countenance.

As I have already consecrated a whole volume, my fifth, *The Mystery of Jesus*, to show how this ought to be done, there is no need of my insisting on the point further than to say that you will grow thereby in the special, personal, distinct knowledge of the second Person of the Blessed Trinity, and, of course, through Him, of His Divine Father and of His Holy Spirit.

Finally, let us suppose that this time—anywheresoever and anywhensoever—it is the Holy Spirit who happens mysteriously to win your loving attention and concentrate it upon Himself personally and for His own sake. Do, then, gaze with all the eagerness of an inflamed soul upon this wonderful third Person of the Blessed Trinity. Talk to Him and hearken to Him, and allow your heart to overflow

WHEN, WHERE, AND HOW

with joy at the sweetness of this meeting. You will come out of it all aglow with experimental knowledge of this Holy Spirit of love, and, of course, also with deeper appreciation of the two first Persons who produce such a marvellous third Person and give Him to you as Their gift.

A beautiful practice, if rather uncommon, and one which may require some delicate discernment, is that of worshipping the Holy Ghost, first in the persons of little baptized children, then in the persons of those adult Christians who lead transparently blameless and fervent lives. Church history relates how the glorious martyr, St. Leonides, was wont during the night reverently to uncover the breast of his youthful son, Origen, whilst he was asleep, and to kiss it as the living, breathing temple of the Holy Spirit. This was genuine mysticism, as much even as the loving kiss given to the lepers by some saints. Only a real mystic could do such an act, and in the right spirit.

Whenever a beautiful act of virtue is performed under our eyes, we ought at once to trace it to its prime author, the

Holy Ghost, and if the act be an heroic one, such as, for instance, setting human respect at naught, forgiving some cruel or even slight injury, but which one keenly resents, bearing in a spirit of faith some great reverse of fortune or loss of dear ones, performing some act of charity against which human nature cannot but revolt, then we ought to discern in this a manifest intervention of the Holy Spirit, and take occasion of it to break forth into rapturous praise of the third Person of the Blessed Trinity.

In my long life of priest and missionary, I have witnessed quite a large number of such manifestations of the Holy Spirit, and it is to me a matter of regret that I did not set them down in writing at the time. They would make fine and edifying reading. One ought to be on the lookout for such occasional flashes, so to say, of the inner fire of the Holy Spirit, burning in the souls of really fervent Christians. Such a habit would serve to offset the pernicious effects which the scandals of the world, in the midst of which we move, have upon us, and about which we are perhaps quite un-

WHEN, WHERE, AND HOW

concerned. I said "fervent Christians." Only with such can we venture to adore the Holy Ghost in them. With the tepid, unedifying, frivolous, and careless, one is never sure whether they are actually in a state of grace. As I have shown in my third volume, *Mysticism, True and False*, it is the misfortune of the tepid Christian to have occasional lapses into mortal sin.

This, then, is my first answer to the questions: When, Where, and How, one may apply oneself to the special worship of each one of the Divine Persons. The answer which I am going to give in the next chapter is the very antithesis of whenever and wherever and however, for it points to set times and circumstances when one is called upon to give particular attention respectively to each one of the Divine Persons.

CHAPTER VI

A Second Answer to the Same Query

SUMMARY.—This comes as a complement to the first answer. We are to pay special attention to God the Father at Mass; for then He fills the Church with His unspeakable Majesty. Also when out of doors, contemplating natural scenery by day or night. To the second Person, when out of Mass, visiting the Blessed Sacrament. *Dominus est.* The eyes of faith discerning Him in the Sacred Host. To the Holy Ghost, when at private prayers and through the day's occupations.

HERE, then, is now the second answer. It comes not as an alternative or a contradiction, but as a complement to the previous one.

First, when are we called upon to pay particular attention to God the Father? I say when we are assisting at the Holy Sacrifice of Mass. This may perhaps surprise unenlightened piety, but a moment's reflection ought to suffice to satisfy anyone as to the soundness of this view. For, indeed, to whom is this sacrifice offered?

A SECOND ANSWER

Is it not to God the Father? The three Divine Persons are there, because they are never separated, but in this solemn act, by the very nature of the function, you are invited to visualize first and foremost God the Father. He it is who at this moment fills the Church with His unspeakable, infinite majesty. To make you realize this fact more vividly you have only to read the Canon of the Mass, especially that part which follows the Consecration down to the Agnus Dei. Then also observe how almost all the Collects, Secrets, and Postcommunions of the Masses the year round are addressed to God the Father. Of course, it may help your piety to think of the millions of blessed angels surrounding the altar at that moment and in silent adoration of the Divine Victim upon it. Still more so, to think of the dear Lord Jesus Himself, there present in flesh and blood, mystically renewing the sacrifice He once offered on Calvary. But, I ask it in all earnestness, were it not a great mistake to forget, to lose sight of, or perhaps, ignore entirely, the principal personage—namely, God the Father, who is at that very moment reconciling to Himself the guilty world, through the blood of His Divine Son, receiving the adorations, thanksgivings, propitiatory prayers and demands of His Divine Son in our behalf?

And yet how many Christians are scarcely conscious of this?

In spite of the progress of the liturgical movement, people are not yet used to reading their Mass-book aright, or to drawing from it for their piety the most obvious lessons. Then, also, as all the rest of the Divine Office by day and night, recited by priests and chanted in choir by monks and nuns, is a prolongation of the Holy Sacrifice of Mass, it is also addressed directly to the first Person of the Blessed Trinity, God the Father—through His Divine Son, of course, in the unity of the Holy Spirit—but first and foremost to God the Father, thus putting us in touch with Him.

We may also most appropriately pay special attention to God the Father and give Him our loving praise, when we happen to be out of doors contemplating the beauties of nature, since the work of creation is, by appropriation, attributed to

A SECOND ANSWER

Him. We ought to look upon the firmament, by day and night, as the most wonderful visible temple built by the Father Himself through the wisdom of the Son by the power of His Holy Spirit—a temple which the Father does indeed fill with the splendour of His infinite Majesty. *Pleni sunt coeli et terra majestatis gloriae tuae.*

We shall have occasion in the sequel of this work to come back upon this consideration. Let this at present suffice as to the proper set time and occasions when it is natural and incumbent upon us to pay special attention to God the Father.

And now, when are we called upon and expected to hold personal intercourse with, and pay special attention to, the second Person of the Blessed Trinity, God the Son? I answer: When, outside the time of the Mass, we are visiting the Blessed Sacrament. Then, indeed, is the time for us to turn all our speech to Him as to *the Son of the Living God*, who eternally proceeds from the Father by way of generation; who is one and the same God with the Father and who, in that oneness, produces with Him, by way of active spiration, the Holy Spirit of Love.

Yes, that small Host, hidden away in the ciborium, shut up behind the golden door of the tabernacle, or perhaps exposed to view in the monstrance for the office of Solemn Benediction or again for the Forty Hours' Devotion, *Dominus est;* it is the Lord, the Lord God, the second Person of the Blessed Three in One; He it is we ought for the moment to visualize by the light of faith, even as though we were with Him and His Apostles on the shores of the Lake of Genesareth, or with Him and His Blessed Angels and Saints in the glory of Paradise. And, of course, as we pay homage to Him, our adoration extends to the Father who eternally begets Him, and to the Holy Spirit whom He, jointly with the Father, is eternally producing.

I and the Father are one (John x, 30), He says—one and the same God—one principle of the Holy Spirit. *My Father worketh until now and I work* (John v, 17), that is to say, the Father is ever begetting His Divine Son, and in His turn the Son

A SECOND ANSWER

is ever producing, in unison with the Father, the Holy Spirit of Love.

When thus engaged in your loving contemplation of the second Person of the Blessed Trinity, then, of course, is also the time of bringing to bear all the affections of your heart upon the sweet mysteries of His sacred Humanity, according to the time of the liturgical year and according to the actual bent of your devotion. I have explained this at great length in my fifth volume, *The Mystery of Jesus*.

Thus will your affective knowledge of the second Person of the Blessed Trinity gain in depth, thereby enhancing also your knowledge and love of the other two Divine Persons.

Finally, as to the Holy Spirit.

Outside of Holy Mass and of the visit to the Blessed Sacrament, when attending to private prayer and to your various occupations through the day, make it a point to address yourself particularly to the third Person of the Blessed Trinity, the Holy Ghost, who is in the living temple of your own body and soul, who is actually sighing after your recognition of the fact, ardently wishing for you to take proper notice of Him and to turn His presence and omnipotent love to your advantage. Will you not adore this Divine Person? Will you not love the very love of the Father and of the Son? Will you not have something to say to this Divine guest and friend and comforter? Will you not find your delight in Him, and through Him in the other two Persons whose Gift He is?

Now, to do this is to enjoy God. To do this is, indeed, to grow in the knowledge and in the love of the Most Holy Trinity.

CHAPTER VII

THE VOICE OF THE BRIDE

SUMMARY.—Many have erred about the doctrine of the Blessed Trinity, because they have neglected the warnings of Holy Writ. My purpose is not to make theologians. No irreverent curiosity, but simple faith and love. The Church has in her sacred liturgy carefully set down the terms in which we ought to think and speak of the Blessed Trinity. Specially in the Nicene Creed and in the Preface of the Mass of the Blessed Trinity.

AFTER reading the three foregoing chapters some might perhaps accuse me of leading those who follow me into dangerous paths.

It is true that many have erred about this fundamental dogma of our faith, the doctrine of the Most Holy Trinity, for having rashly ventured to scrutinize the depths of the mystery, when they should have been satisfied with believing and adoring.

Such men did not bear enough in mind the caution given by Proverbs thus: *As it is not good for a man to eat much honey, so he that is a searcher of majesty, shall be overwhelmed by glory* (Prov. xxv, 27). Nor again the warning of Ecclesiasticus: *Seek not the things that are too high for thee, and search not into things that are above thy ability; but the things that God hath commanded thee, think of them always, and in many of His works be not curious; for it is not necessary for thee to see with thy eyes those things which are hid* (Eccli. iii, 22, 23).

Now, in self-defence, I protest that my purpose is not to make theologians of my readers, recruited as they are from all ranks of the Christian commonwealth, from the humblest as well as from the middle ranks and from the highest.

No, not theologians in the common acceptation of this word; not theologians, but what is far better, adorers of God *in spirit and truth* (John iv, 23). This all may certainly desire and strive after, as they are sweetly invited to do by Our Lord, were they even such as the poor, ill-educated, ignorant and sinful Samaritan woman who met Him at Jacob's well.

The contemplative soul does not

THE VOICE OF THE BRIDE

approach the infinite Majesty and Sanctity of God with irreverent curiosity, but with humble faith and love. She is thankful that Holy Mother Church has carefully set down the terms within which we are safe to think and speak of the Most Holy Trinity. This the Church has done throughout the whole range of her sacred liturgy, but more particularly in two wonderful official documents, the Nicene Creed, and the Preface of the Mass of the Blessed Trinity, including the Trisagion which follows.

Every Christian ought to be able to find these in his Sunday Mass-book: nevertheless, for the sake of completeness, we subjoin them here, dividing them into paragraphs and italicising the important words, so as to help the mind of the reader to take in their full import and co-ordination. Thus it will be easier to understand why the Church, the Bride of Christ, makes the Nicene Creed an hymn of triumph, bringing as it does to the Apostles' Creed, after hard conflicts, the precisions and developments which the first heresies had rendered necessary.

THE BURNING BUSH

As to the Preface, no one needs to be told that it is one of the sublimest lyrical outbursts of the spirit of adoration, at the same time as an absolutely scientific statement of the terms of the mystery of the Blessed Trinity. A rare combination, indeed, and one which could not be accounted for but by the direct assistance and inspiration of the Holy Spirit.

That is what I call the voice of the Bride.

I.—THE NICENE CREED.

I believe in one God,
the Father Almighty,
Maker of Heaven and Earth,
of all things visible and invisible.

And in One Lord Jesus Christ,
The only-begotten Son of God and born of the Father before all ages; God of God, light of light, true God of true God: begotten, not made, consubstantial with the Father, by whom all things were made.

Who for us men, and for our salvation, came down from heaven, and was incarnate by the Holy Spirit, of the Virgin Mary, and was made man.

He was crucified also for us, under Pontius Pilate, He suffered and was buried.

The third day He rose again according to the Scriptures, and ascended into heaven and sitteth on the right hand of the Father, and shall come again with glory to judge the living and the dead.

Of whose Kingdom there shall be no end.

And in the Holy Ghost,
The Lord and Life-Giver, who proceedeth from the Father and the Son; who together with the Father and Son is adored and glorified, who spoke by the Prophets.

And one, Holy, Catholic, Apostolic Church. I confess one baptism for the remission of sins.

And I look for the resurrection of the dead and the life of the world to come. Amen.

II.—The Preface of the Trinity with the Trisagion.

It is truly meet and just, right and salutary that we should, at all times and in all places, give thanks unto Thee.

THE BURNING BUSH

Holy Lord, Father Almighty, Everlasting God, who together with Thine only-begotten Son and the Holy Ghost art one God and one Lord,

Not in the singleness of one person,
But in the Trinity of one substance.

For that which by Thy revelation we believe of Thy glory, the same also we hold as to Thy Son, the same as to the Holy Spirit, without difference or distinction.

That in the confession of the true and everlasting Godhead,

Distinction in Persons,
Unity in Essence,
And equality in Majesty may be adored.
Which the Angels and Archangels,
The Cherubim also and Seraphim praise, *who cease not daily to cry out with one voice, saying:*

Holy, Holy, Holy, is the Lord God of Hosts,
Full are the heavens and the earth of Thy glory.
Hosanna in the heights!

There are many other liturgical texts, such as, for instance, the so-called *Athan-*

asian Creed, the *Gloria in Excelsis Deo*, the *Te Deum Laudamus*, and an immense variety of Doxologies, which may be pressed into service by the contemplative soul, but the two we have just given will suffice to supply, at least, the framework, so to say, and the keynote for practically endless considerations and affections on the great mystery.

This whole book of mine has no other pretension than to be some kind of unconventional paraphrase of these two wonderful formulas of the Catholic faith and love, the Nicene Creed and the Preface of the Mass of the Blessed Trinity.

CHAPTER VIII

THE MYSTERY OF THE FATHER

SUMMARY.—It is the mystery of the Divine Life which the Father lives within Himself, the Divine operations He performs, the Divine Persons He produces. God speaks His Word. Despair of the man who would express God and love Him adequately. What man cannot do God does. Saying that God is the creator of heaven and earth gives no idea of what God is in Himself, but the Mystery of the Father does.

UNTO the knowledge of the mystery of the Father (Col. ii, 2).

The mystery of the Father, what is it?

It is that from all eternity He is begetting a Son, His own living Image: and that this Eternal Father and this Eternal Son do so love each other that, in the act of breathing out their mutual love, they eternally produce a third Divine Person, their Holy Spirit. The mystery of the Father is the mystery of the Divine life He lives within Himself, of the Divine opera-

THE MYSTERY OF THE FATHER

tions He performs within Himself, of the Divine Persons He produces.

One would like to speak worthily of God, to express Him magnificently, adequately, to speak Him out to one's fellow-men in our human language, the only one at hand, in a way that would truly set Him before their eyes. Alas! this is absolutely impossible. Seeing which, the servant of God would fain, even as John in the Apocalypse, when he discovered that no one could open the book with the seven seals, break out into tears (Apoc. v, 4).

Fain would he remain disconsolate, were it not that a voice whispers to him as one of the Ancients to John: *Weep not* (Apoc. v, 5). Weep not; for what no man can do the Lord Himself does: He speaks one word, only one word, His Word, His own Divine Word, and thereby expresses Himself fully, magnificently, adequately. It takes God to speak worthily of God. Now He does it: He does it from all eternity.

My God, I give Thee thanks! O Eternal Father, I give Thee thanks! And to Thee also, O Divine Word, I give rapturous thanks! Here, then, is the mystery of the Father beginning to unravel itself before our gaze. Let us be bold: let us proceed: let us push forward unto the loving contemplation of the mystery of the Father.

One could wish to love God the Father and His Divine Son as one conceives that such a Father and such a Son are worthy to be loved. Alas! that is absolutely impossible to the creature.

Seeing which, the servant of God again might break his heart, but here also a voice tells him: *Weep not*. Weep not: for what neither thou, nor any creature, or any number of creatures put together could ever achieve, God does perfectly in one single act: God loves God adequately, God loves God even as God deserves to be loved; God the Father loves His Son, His living Image, His Word, who expresses Him so magnificently—He loves Him, I say, to the absolutely full measure of His deserving. And in His turn, God the Son loves the Divine Father, from whom He receives all that He has and is—He loves Him, I say, to the full measure of

THE MYSTERY OF THE FATHER

His deserving, that is to say, infinitely. And in Their mutual infinite love, the Father and the Son breathe out the third Divine Person, the Holy Spirit.

Oh, thanks, my God, Holy Trinity: I give Thee thanks *propter magnam gloriam tuam*, that Thou art thus One God in three Divine Persons; the Lover, the Loved One, the Love: "Amans, Amatus, Amor" as one of the ancient Fathers of the Church has most felicitously expressed it.

This, then, is the mystery of the Father: that God is Love; *Deus caritas est;* God is love in three Divine Persons. This is the mystery that the Father eternally carries in His bosom, which the Son came down upon earth to reveal to us, and which the Holy Spirit brings to pass, even into our very heart and soul and flesh.

When we are told that God is the creator of Heaven and earth, it does not give us to understand what God is. True, none but God could create anything whatever; but God would no less be what He is had He never created anything.

But when we are told that God is the Blessed Trinity of the Father and of the

THE BURNING BUSH

Son and of the Holy Ghost, we come by faith, unto the knowledge of the mystery of the Divine Life and its ineffable operations. The world of creatures is outside the Divine Essence, but the Son is *in the Father's bosom* and is God; then we begin to know God from the inside even as He is in Himself: we come *unto the knowledge of the mystery of the Father*.

The Father is the headspring of the Divine Essence, He is *la Divinité—Source* (*Fons Deitatis*).

O glory be to the Father!

Glory be to the Father through the Son!

Glory be to the Father through the Son, in the unity of the Holy Spirit. Amen. Amen. Amen.

CHAPTER IX

More about God the Father

SUMMARY.—How this should be understood. Whatever is said of the other two Persons and of the Divine Nature as such makes us know more of the Father. The Collects of the Mass. The sayings of Our Lord in the Gospel. How a devotional treatise could be made on this entrancing subject.

TO speak of "more about the Father" is a very human way of expressing ourselves. For, indeed, when we have stated that He is the Father and has ever with Him His Divine Son and His Holy Spirit of Love, all is said completely, adequately.

All is said: yes; but all is not apprehended by our puny minds. It remains for us to open, so to speak, and to unfold this theological statement, and to perceive as distinctly as will be given us all that lies hidden therein, and to give due praise to God the Father for all this.

THE BURNING BUSH

It must be owned that God the Father is the one of the three Divine Persons to whom most Christians give least attention.

The second Person being Our Lord Jesus Christ, so near to us by means of His Sacred Humanity, arrests our attention much more and almost monopolizes it; though we give also, at least from time to time, some thought to the Holy Ghost. But God the Father, although we are made to name Him first in our every sign of the Cross and every doxology, we can hardly say that we bestow any thought upon Him.

Now this is not all as it should be, nor, indeed, as our Lord and Holy Mother Church would have it.

It is true that whosoever honours any one of the three Divine Persons, implicitly honours, at the same time, the other two; but such implicit worship ought not to satisfy our piety. Both our Lord in the Gospel, and Holy Church in the sacred liturgy, tell us a great deal about God the Father, evidently with a view to lead us into making much of Him.

Unfortunately this twofold, very earnest

teaching, most of the time, falls upon inattentive ears. Out of sheer fickleness of mind, men, as a rule, will not give to the First Person what they owe Him, and their piety is impoverished in proportion.

Let us realize that just as it is a sign of a high spiritual life to cultivate an explicit, felt, conscious devotion to the Blessed Trinity, so also is it a sign of real spiritual progress when we come to have a great and enlightened love for the Person of God the Father in particular.

A more explicit and fervent love of the Father, far from diminishing our love of Our Lord, will rather intensify and deepen it, by making it more intelligent, better informed, more theological, more real.

First of all, it must be understood that all we are going to say in subsequent chapters about the Son and the Holy Ghost will make us know more of the Father. This is obvious. It will make us know more, and more distinctly, His inner life, with His Divine operations of which these two other Persons are the results. The better we know the Son and the Holy Ghost, the richer, if we will only reflect, grows our knowledge of Him who produces them.

Then (and this may sound like a repetition of what we have just been saying, but it is not) it must also be understood that it is impossible to say anything in praise of the Divine Nature as such, without its resulting, in a most particular way, in praise of God the Father, thereby further enhancing our knowledge of Him; because of His being the headspring from which is derived all that belongs to the Divine Nature, as well as all things created. This has been admirably set forth in the celebrated text of St. James: *Every best gift and every perfect gift is from above, coming down from the Father of lights, with whom there is no change nor shadow of alteration* (James i, 17), His *best gift* being His Divine Son, for it is written: *God so loved the world as to give it His only-begotten Son* (John iii, 16), and His *perfect gift* being His Holy Ghost, for Our Lord said to His Apostles: *I will ask the Father, and He shall give you another Paraclete, that He may be with you for ever, the Spirit of Truth* (John xiv, 16, 17). Could a more

MORE ABOUT GOD THE FATHER

perfect gift ever be thought of? And now, does not all this increase our knowledge of the goodness of the Father?

In the same strain does St. Paul exclaim: *To us there is but one God, the Father, of whom are all things and we unto Him* (1 Cor. viii, 6)—and again: *Blessed be God the Father of Our Lord Jesus Christ, the Father of mercies and the God of all comfort* (2 Cor. i, 3).

We may note also that in all the Masses of the liturgical cycle, the Collects, Secrets, and Post-communions being generally addressed to the Father, they tell us of Him, they mention explicitly some of His Divine perfections.

Finally, do we want still further and still more distinctly to know the Father, we have the short, pregnant sentences of Our Lord about Him in the Gospel, wherein we may find an inexhaustible theme for our pious meditations and ecstatic contemplation. For has not Jesus said: *No one knoweth who the Father is but the Son, and he to whom the Son will reveal Him* (Luke x, 22)—and again: *No man cometh to the Father*, and consequently to the knowledge of the Father, *but by Me* (John xiv, 6)—and again to the Jews: *If you did know Me perhaps you would know My Father also* (John viii, 19).

In this connection perhaps I may be permitted to mention that I had thought of collecting and paraphrasing briefly all the texts of the New Testament where God the Father is mentioned. I thought this would make an illuminating chapter to this present book. Illuminating no doubt it would have been, but I soon had to stop, for I discovered that not one chapter only, but at least one more volume, possibly even two would have to be made out of such a rich harvest of Scripture materials. Now, much as I would like to add this new labour of love to my other works, I am not prepared, nor indeed at liberty, to open such a wide parenthesis in the series of my treatises on Traditional Mysticism, which is not near completion. I can only recommend this interesting side-enterprise to anyone who might have the courage to do it for his own spiritual delight and edification. No telling but that this would even be the making of him as a writer and that he would eventually enrich the world with a precious and beautiful new treatise at once theological and devotional.

Without aiming quite so high as that, any priest or student of theology, or pious educated layman, would certainly increase his knowledge and love of God the Father by simply taking the trouble to look up for himself in his New Testament and to mark, let us say, with red ink, all the passages which refer to the first Person of the Blessed Trinity, so that he might at any moment lay his hand upon some of them and meditate upon them in a spirit of prayer.

CHAPTER X

THE WORD, THE SECOND PERSON OF THE BLESSED TRINITY

SUMMARY.—A new theological expression peculiar to St. John. Silence of the other writers of the New Testament in this regard. The same appellation is found with the identical meaning of St. John, in several passages of the Old Testament, though it does not appear that the inspired writers of that time, still less the bulk of the People of God, understood its full import.

HAVING now to speak of the second Person of the Blessed Trinity, it becomes necessary to premise a few remarks about the fourth Gospel, that of St. John. It is therein that we find for the first time in the New Testament the peculiar and highly significant new appellation of THE WORD—along with His proper name of the Only-begotten Son—by which this second Person is already known to us. St. John is the only one of the inspired writers of the New Testament to make use of this expression in this sense. None of

THE WORD

the three synoptic evangelists, Matthew, Mark, and Luke, nor any of the other writers of the canonical epistles, Peter, James, and Jude, nor St. Paul the Apostle of the Gentiles, ever use the term "Word of God" with any other meaning than the common one of a sound uttered by the lips or the written sign of it. St. John is the only one who uses it as the proper appellation of the very Son of God; and he introduces it in the Scripture vocabulary with such a splendour, such a magnificent insistence and display of pomp and ceremony, if we may say so, that we cannot fail to notice its novelty and paramount importance.

Here are the opening sentences of his Gospel: *In the beginning was the Word, and the Word was with God, and the Word was God. The same was in the beginning with God. All things were made by Him, and without Him was made nothing that was made. In Him was life and the life was the light of men . . . the true light which enlighteneth every man that cometh into the world. . . . And the Word was made flesh and dwelt among us (and we saw His glory, the glory as it were of the only-begotten of the Father) full of grace and truth* (John i, 1-4, 9, 14).

The opening sentence of the first canonical epistle of the same St. John is no less sublime, insistent, and explicit in its identification of *the Word* with the second Person of the Blessed Trinity:

That which was from the beginning, which we have heard, which we have seen with our eyes, which we have looked upon and our hands have handled of the Word of life—for the life was manifested and we have seen and do bear witness, and declare unto you the life eternal which was with the Father and hath appeared to us—that which we have seen and have heard, we declare unto you, that you may have fellowship with us, and our fellowship may be with the Father, and with His Son Jesus Christ (1 John i, 1-3).

This epistle, according to the latest conclusions of exegesis, was evidently written by St. John as a sort of Preface and parenthetical commentary to his Gospel, and must have been sent together with it to different Churches, so that we may well

THE WORD

consider it as forming a unique document with this Gospel.

The silence of the other inspired writers of the New Testament about the Word of God as the second Person of the Blessed Trinity is the more remarkable in that the Old Testament supplies us with several striking passages where the expression *the Word of God* is so used, that, with the knowledge we now have of the mystery of the Blessed Trinity, we can apply it but to a Divine Person. Thus in the Book of Wisdom:

While all things were in quiet silence, and the night was in the midst of her course, Thy Almighty Word leapt down from heaven from the royal throne as a conqueror into the midst of the land of destruction, with a sharp sword carrying Thy unfeigned commandment, and He stood and filled all things with death, and standing on the earth, reached even unto heaven (Wisd. xviii, 14-16).

It were difficult not to see in this magnificent description a Divine Person, proceeding from God, "God of God" as the Nicene Creed puts it, *omnipotent*, even as He who sent Him, therefore co-equal to Him. The sacred liturgy appropriates the first three lines of the above text to the Introit of the Mass of the Sunday within the Octave of Christmas, thus applying these words to the mystery of the Incarnation, to the Person of Our Lord, God made man.

Then again in Psalm cvi, 19-20:
They cried to the Lord in their affliction, and he delivered them out of their distresses.
He sent His Word and healed them and delivered them from their destructions.
How marvellously literally does this passage apply to the mission of the second Person by the Father, in the mystery of the Incarnation and to His subsequent work of our salvation! This shows that what is said here of the Israelites was only a prophetic figure of what was to be enacted in our behalf by Our Lord, the great Healer and Deliverer and Restorer, therefore there can be no doubt but that it is here really a question of the second Person of the Blessed Trinity.

THE WORD

Again in Psalm xxxii, 6 we read:

By the word of the Lord the heavens were established, and all the power of them by the spirit of His mouth.

The Fathers of the Church are unanimous in seeing in this verse an express mention of the Three Persons of the Blessed Trinity: the Lord, His Word, and the Holy Spirit: the express name of *the Word* being given to the second Person.

A very striking parallel can be established between several passages of the Sapiential books on the one hand and the Johannine statements as to the Word who was made flesh on the other.

Thus in Ecclesiasticus i, v. 1 we read:

All wisdom is from the Lord God and has been always with Him and is before all time. And in ch. i, 5: *The word of God on high is the fountain of wisdom.*

In Proverbs (i, 20-23; viii, 1-36; ix, 1-7) wisdom is a person, not a mere abstract concept or an empty word, or a purely figurative expression—a real person, nay, a Divine Person. All that St. John in the first verses of his Gospel sings of *the*

Word can be and must be attributed to *Wisdom* as she reveals herself to us in the book that bears her very name and in those of Proverbs and Ecclesiasticus. She speaks, she acts, she is *in God*, she plays before Him and *delights to come among the sons of men*, and walks with them *full of grace and truth*.

And yet it must be owned that, for all the magnificent explicitness of these diverse passages as to the Divine Wisdom or the Divine Word being a distinct Divine Person, it does not appear that any of the inspired sacred writers of that time, still less the bulk of the then People of God, understood their full import. If they did understand it at the time, the tradition of such an interpretation did not last long enough to make a deep impression. It had completely vanished at the time of Our Lord; so much so that the main accusation of the Pharisees against Him was that He proclaimed Himself a Divine Person distinct from the Father. They encompassed His death on the very charge that He had blasphemed by proclaiming Himself the Son of God. Our Lord is the King of Martyrs on that very score, that He laid down His life in defence of the dogma of His Divine Sonship.

But of this more in the next chapter.

CHAPTER XI

The Only-Begotten Son

SUMMARY.—That the second Person proceeds from the first by way of generation. Testimony of the Father, of the Son, of the Holy Spirit.

IN the course of a most moving description of the Passion of Christ, one of the prophets exclaims: *His generation who shall declare?* (Is. liii, 8).

Who indeed? For to do this is beyond the capacity of any created intellect whether human or angelical. Therefore on so sublime a subject we do not want to say anything of our own. God Himself will declare it to us—God the Father, and God the Son, and God the Holy Ghost—God the Father in many passages of both the Old and the New Testament, God the Son all through His Divine Gospel, God the Holy Ghost by the mouth of the Catholic Church in the formularies of the Faith and throughout her sacred liturgy. Says St.

THE ONLY-BEGOTTEN SON

John in his first epistle (1 John v, 7): *There are three who give testimony in heaven, the Father, the Word, and the Holy Ghost.*

Of course, we shall have to make a choice among the immense number of these varied testimonies; but the few to which we shall restrict ourselves will amply suffice for our purpose.

The pious reader who is desirous of drawing from this rather long chapter all the spiritual profit possible, will be well advised to read it by small instalments, slowly, prayerfully. Give an opportunity to the Holy Ghost to open the ears and the eyes of your understanding and to inflame your heart. And when you have thus read this chapter a first time and for its own sake, you may perhaps increase your spiritual gain twofold by reading it a second time, in connection with Chapter X of my fifth volume, *The Mystery of Jesus*, which is all about the two nativities of Christ, the one from the Father, from all eternity, the other from the Virgin-Mother, in the fulness of time.

THE BURNING BUSH

THE TESTIMONY OF THE FATHER.

In Isaias we read: *Shall not I that make others to bring forth children Myself bring forth, saith the Lord? Shall I that give generation to others be barren, saith the Lord thy God?* (Is. lxvi, 9).

David, raised in spirit in heaven, hears one Divine Person (Dominus) saying to another Divine Person (Domino meo): *Sit Thou at My right hand until I make Thine enemies Thy footstool . . . In the splendours of holiness from the womb, before the day star I begot Thee* (Ps. cix, 1-3).

The same David in Psalm ii sings the glories of the Lord and His Christ whom he introduces saying: *The Lord God hath said to me: thou art My son, this day have I begotten thee;* and further down he gives this exhortation (Hebrew text): *Kiss the Son, lest at any time the Lord be angry and you perish from the just way* (Ps. ii, 7, 12).

Jesus being baptized . . . lo, the heavens were opened . . . and behold a voice from

THE ONLY-BEGOTTEN SON

heaven saying: *This is My beloved Son, in whom I am well pleased* (Matt. iii, 16, 17).

He was transfigured before (Peter, James, and John), *and behold, a bright cloud overshadowed them, and lo, a voice out of the cloud saying: This is My beloved Son in whom I am well pleased; hear ye Him* (Matt. xvii, 2, 5).

To Peter who made this solemn profession of faith: *Thou art Christ, the Son of the Living God,* our Lord said: *Blessed art thou, Simon Bar-Jona, because flesh and blood hath not revealed it to thee, but My Father who is in heaven* (Matt. xvi, 16, 17).

When certain Gentiles came to Philip saying: *Sir, we would see Jesus.* . . . Jesus answered them saying: *The hour is come that the Son of Man should be glorified.* . . . *Now is my soul troubled, and what shall I say?* . . . *Father glorify Thy Name. A voice therefore came from heaven: I have both glorified it and will glorify it again* (John xii, 20, 23, 27, 28).

THE BURNING BUSH

In the first chapter of his wonderful epistle to the Hebrews, St. Paul writes:

God who at sundry times and in diverse manners spoke, in past times, to the fathers by the prophets, last of all in these days hath spoken to us by the Son, whom He hath appointed heir of all things, by whom also He made the world; who being the brightness of His glory and the figure of His substance and upholding all things by the word of His power, making purgation of sins, sitteth on the right hand of the majesty on high, being made so much better than the angels as He hath inherited a more excellent name than they (Heb. i, 1-4).

THE TESTIMONY OF THE SON.

Luke ii, 46-49. It came to pass that after these days they found Him sitting in the temple in the midst of the doctors, hearing them and asking them questions: and all that heard Him were astonished at His wisdom and His answers.... And His mother said to Him: Son, why hast Thou done so to us? Behold Thy father and I have sought Thee sorrowing. And He said to them: How is it that you sought

THE ONLY-BEGOTTEN SON

Me? Did you not know that I must be about My Father's business?

To Nicodemus, who had come to Him secretly, at night, Jesus said, among other striking revelations about Himself and His mission:

God so loved the world as to give His only-begotten Son; that whosoever believeth in Him, may not perish, but may have life everlasting.

For God sent not His Son into the world to judge the world, but that the world may be saved by Him. He that believeth in Him is not judged, but he that doth not believe is already judged, because he believeth not in the name of the only-begotten Son of God.

When Our Lord had healed, on the Sabbath day, the man who had been languishing thirty-eight years, the Jews persecuted Him. But Jesus answered them: *My Father worketh until now and I work.*

Hereupon therefore the Jews sought the more to kill Him, because He did not only

THE BURNING BUSH

break the Sabbath, but also said God was His Father, making Himself equal to God. Then Jesus answered and said to them: *Amen, amen, I say unto you, the Son cannot do anything of Himself, but what He seeth the Father doing: for what things soever He doeth, these the Son also doth in like manner. For the Father loveth the Son, and showeth Him all things which Himself doth. . . .*

For as the Father raiseth up the dead and giveth life, so also the Son giveth life to whom He will . . . that all men may honour the Son as they honour the Father. . . . Amen, amen, I say unto you that he who heareth My voice and believeth Him that sent Me, hath life everlasting. . . . The Father Himself who hath sent Me hath given testimony of Me (John v).

In the course of the passionate altercation which fills the eighth chapter of St. John's Gospel, the Jews said to Our Lord:

We have one Father, even God. Jesus therefore said to them: If God were your Father you would indeed love Me. For from God I proceeded, and came: for I

THE ONLY-BEGOTTEN SON

came not of Myself, but He sent Me. Abraham your father rejoiced that he might see My day: he saw it and was glad. The Jews therefore said to Him: Thou art not yet fifty years old, and hast thou seen Abraham? Jesus said unto them: Amen, amen, I say to you, before Abraham was made, I am.

They took up stones therefore to cast at Him, but Jesus hid Himself and went out of the temple.

At the feast of the Dedication at Jerusalem, Jesus walked in the temple in Solomon's porch, and, to the Jews who came round about Him, He said among other things: *I and the Father are one.*

As was to be expected, in His discourse at the Last Supper, which is such an entrancing effusion of the love of His heart to His Apostles, Our Lord gives many most explicit testimonies of His Divine Sonship. Chapters xiii to xvii of St. John should be read attentively from this point of view. For brevity's sake we shall retain but the following passages:

THE BURNING BUSH

In My Father's house there are many mansions (John xiv, 2)—*No man cometh to the Father but by Me* (ibid., xiv, 6)—*Philip, he that seeth Me, seeth the Father also* (ibid., 9)—*The word which you have heard is not Mine, but the Father's who sent Me* (ibid., 24)—*Amen, amen, I say to you, if you ask the Father anything in My Name, He will give it you* (xvi, 23).

I came forth from the Father, and am come into the world; again I leave the world and go to the Father (xvi, 28).

Father, the hour is come, glorify Thy Son that Thy Son may glorify Thee (xvii, 1).

I pray that they all may be one, as Thou Father in Me and I in Thee, that they also may be one in Us, that the world may believe Thou hast sent Me (xvii, 21).

Father, I will that where I am they also whom Thou hast given Me may be with Me, that they may see My glory which Thou hast given Me, because Thou hast loved Me before the creation of the world (xvii, 24).

He that could read these words of self-revelation uttered by the Son of God under the circumstances which we know without

THE ONLY-BEGOTTEN SON

being moved to admiration and intensest love must be very dull indeed.

We come now to the wonderful scene in His sacred Passion, when Our Lord gave the supreme testimony as to His Divine Sonship, that of the sacrifice of His life. It is in a way the grandest page of all the Holy Scriptures, and should be read on our knees, with deepest feelings of adoration of His Divine Majesty and tears of sorrow for our sins. Picture Him in your mind's eye as best you can, standing before the High Priest—His Hands bound as a criminal—silent, calm, majestic.

Last of all came two false witnesses and they said: This Man said, I am able to destroy the temple of God, and after three days to rebuild it. And the High Priest said to Him: Answerest Thou nothing to these things which these witness against Thee? But Jesus held His peace.

And the High Priest said to Him: I adjure Thee, by the living God, that Thou tell us if Thou be Christ, the Son of God.

Jesus saith to him:

Thou hast said it. Nevertheless I say to

you, hereafter you shall see the Son of Man sitting on the right hand of the power of God and coming in the clouds of heaven.

Then the High Priest rent his garments, saying: He hath blasphemed: what further need have we of witnesses? Behold, now you have heard the blasphemy: what think you?

But they answering said: He is guilty of death (Matt. xxvi, 60-67).

TESTIMONY OF THE HOLY SPIRIT

In the Apostles' Creed:

"I believe in God the Father . . . and in Jesus Christ, His *only-begotten Son*."

In the Nicene Creed:

"I believe in God the Father . . . and in the Lord Jesus Christ, the only-begotten Son of God, and *born of the Father before all ages:* God of God, light of light, true God of true God, begotten not made, consubstantial with the Father, by whom all things were made."

In the Athanasian Creed:

"The Son is *from the Father alone*, not made, not created, but *begotten*. . . .

THE ONLY-BEGOTTEN SON

"Our Lord Jesus Christ the Son of God is God and man.

"He is God, *begotten before all ages*, of the substance of the Father, and He is man, born in time of the substance of His Mother, a perfect God and a perfect man, made up of a rational soul and human flesh: equal to the Father in the Godhead, inferior to the Father in His humanity, who, although God and Man, is not two but one only Christ; one indeed, not that the Godhead has been changed in Him into flesh, but because His human nature has been assumed into the Godhead: absolutely one, not by a mixture of the substance, but by the oneness of Person, for, just as a human soul and body make a man, so also God and man make one Christ."

Almost all the prayers of the sacred liturgy are addressed to God the Father and concluded in this set form: "*through Our Lord Jesus Christ, Thy Son*, who liveth and reigneth with Thee in the unity of the Holy Spirit, world without end."

Other prayers, comparatively few in number, which are addressed directly to

THE BURNING BUSH

Our Lord, have a conclusion which by implication proclaims as clearly as the above His Divine Sonship, thus: "Who livest and reignest with God the Father in the unity of the Holy Spirit, world without end."

Though in this chapter our sole purpose has been to put before the reader the dogma of the procession of the second Person from the First by way of Filiation, still it has not been advisable in the above extracts from the Creeds to separate what is said about the mystery of the Incarnation: the quotation would have appeared too badly mutilated.

Besides, what is mentioned of the mystery of the Incarnation, incidentally and by contrast, helps to set forth the Divine Filiation in bolder relief.

CHAPTER XII

How St. John came by the Expression "The Word"

SUMMARY.—He did not borrow it from Greek lore, but it was revealed to him straight from heaven. The Logos of Hellenic literature is an abstraction; that of St. John and of the Old Testament, a living and Divine Person. Striking corollary.

MODERNIST writers, and, I am sorry to say, even some Catholic ones, are at great pains to explain how St. John came by this wonderful expression *The Word*, in Latin *Verbum*, in Greek *Logos*, meaning thereby the second Person of the Blessed Trinity.

We need not trace it to St. John's borrowing from Greek literature. All we need to do is just read attentively a few verses of the Apocalypse. There the riddle is solved for us most satisfactorily. The idea of the Logos—word and all—was revealed to St. John straight from heaven.

Listen: *And I saw heaven open, and*

THE BURNING BUSH

behold a white horse, and He that sat upon it was called Faithful and True, and with justice doth He judge and fight. And His eyes were as a flame of fire, and on His head were many diadems, and He had a name written which no man knoweth but Himself and He was clothed with a garment sprinkled with blood, and His name is called the Word of God (Apocalypsis xix, 11, 13).

Is this clear enough and express enough? *And His name is called* THE WORD OF GOD. See how well the description fits our Lord. *The white horse* is the image of the immaculate flesh of His sacred Humanity; *He that sat upon it* is the image of His Human Soul, Faithful and True, indeed, and oh! how valiant in the fight against sin and the powers of darkness! Hence the *many diadems* that are on *His Head;* hence also *His garment sprinkled with blood.* But what is that mysterious name which until then no man knew but Himself? Here it is at last revealed: *And His name is called the Word of God.*

There is no middle course left for us but either to range ourselves with the rationalists who, whenever they come upon such luminous texts, invariably shut their eyes in order not to see them—or to walk with the humble believers (so much more reasonable than the rationalists), who gladly receive the light of Divine revelation and adore it.

Yes, the expression the *Word of God* came to St. John straight from heaven, and this ought to make us cease to be surprised at the sublimity of the beginning of the fourth Gospel.

This St. John wrote, as is now well established, not before but after the grand revelation of the Apocalypse; and the same is true, no doubt, of his wonderful first epistle. Previous to that, he had been, during Domitian's persecution, condemned to death, and had, in consequence, suffered martyrdom by being immersed in a tank of boiling oil, though he had been miraculously kept alive, nay, he had come out of this terrible ordeal endowed with renewed vigour. Then he had been exiled in the island of Patmos and there it was that he had the grand visions related in the last book of the canon of the Holy Scriptures.

THE BURNING BUSH

It is natural to conjecture that, after the particular vision related above, St. John was full of the thought of Our Lord as the Word of God. He thought of Him constantly under this novel aspect, freighted with glorious meaning, and by Divine inspiration his meditation blossomed out in those wonderful first verses of both his Gospel and his first epistle.

Until then he had known Our Lord, indeed, as the *Son of the living God*, as *the Lord*, as the Friend with the wonderful loving heart, as the Redeemer, as the Conqueror of death and sin, and the One seated at the right hand of God in glory: but now he is taken and he takes us with himself into the very heart of the Blessed Trinity. He is made to contemplate and to reveal to us the pure Divinity of Jesus, and all this is borne upon us along with the God-given, God-revealed, new name of *the Word*.

From this it follows that, much as it may seem to agree with the Greek concept of the Logos of Plato and Philo, we must not see in the expression "the Word," applied by St. John to the second Person of the Blessed

"THE WORD"

Trinity, a felicitous adaptation from the Hellenic philosophy.

That to a limited extent the "Logos" of the Greeks and "the Word" of St. John should convey identical meaning seems to me a pure coincidence, though a very happy one, for it must have made it more easy for the Greeks to accept the Gospel of St. John. The rich Hellenic expression "Logos" conveys a wonderful multiplicity of meanings, such as those of word, idea, truth, wisdom, order, the reason of things, measure, beauty; but all these in Greek literature are mere abstractions. Not so in our Gospel of St. John, nor for that matter in the passages quoted in the preceding chapter, from the Sapiential Books of the Old Testament. The Word there is a living entity proceeding from the Supreme Living Entity, God the Father, One with Him and with the Holy Spirit, in fact the *Actus Purus*. He is *The Life*, the Uncreated Life, the fountain-head of all created life; and also *The Light*, the very light of God, the light by which the Father sees His Divine Self and all things else, past, present, or future and all things that are merely possible; and *He is also the very light which enlighteneth every man that cometh into the world.*

Now see what this means for each one of us. Follow my reasoning and apply it to yourself.

I seek out for myself before my birth, before the first ancestors of our race, before the very dawn of creation, and I find myself in the Word of God, in that wonderful reservoir or store-room of all the Divine ideas. There am I, a thing that will be, whose idea is adumbrated, nay, well defined; whose realization is freely, if irrevocably, decided upon; and it is He, the Word of God, who will, in due time, bring me into actual existence, and not only me, but as well everything else which shall ever have the tiniest particle of life. *All things were made by Him, and without Him was made nothing that was made* (John i, 3).

O Word of the Father, O Wisdom of the Father, O splendour and loveliness of the Father, second Person of the Most Holy Trinity! Thee I love, and adore rapturously —Thee and the Father who begets Thee,

"*THE WORD*"

and the Holy Spirit who receives from the Father and from Thee; I confess Thou art the very light which enlighteneth the eyes of my weak understanding. Oh! when shall I see Thee as Thou art in Thy Father's bosom?

CHAPTER XIII

The Wonders of the Third Person

SUMMARY.—The Holy Ghost was known as a Divine Person by Mary and Joseph, though not by the People of God in the Old Testament. Danger of our conceiving the Holy Ghost as somehow inferior to the Father and the Son. Precisions formulated in the Athanasian Creed. Personal characteristic of the Holy Ghost: He is the substantial sweetness of the Divine Essence. Testimony of Our Lord about Him. Fecundity of the Holy Ghost. How we stand in regard to Him.

IN the historical accounts of the mystery of the Incarnation given respectively in the first chapter of St. Luke and in the first of St. Matthew, we see that both the Blessed Virgin Mary and St. Joseph understood at once who the Holy Ghost was, to whom the operation of the mystery was attributed—namely, a Divine Person.

Although express mention of the *Spirit of the Lord* is so often made throughout the Old Testament, it does not appear that the People of God had any notion that the expression meant anything more than a Divine attribute, that, in fact, it meant a Divine Person. This revelation was reserved for the fulness of time when Christ, the Son of God, should be born; and Mary, His Virgin Mother, was the first to whom it was made. To Mary's query: *How shall this be done, because I know not man? the angel answering said: The Holy Ghost shall come upon thee, and the power of the Most High shall overshadow thee; and therefore the Holy which shall be born of thee shall be called the Son of God* (Luke i, 34, 35). Thus was for the first time the Holy Ghost revealed in His true character of the third of a Blessed Trinity of Divine Persons, of whom the Son of God is the second, and the Father the first; thus for the first time was the whole mystery of the Blessed Trinity explicitly unfolded.

The Holy Ghost is a Person, a Divine Person, the third of the Divine Persons in the unity of the Divine Essence.

There may lurk in the mind of some Christians an impression, certainly unconscious and unformulated, that the Holy

Ghost is somehow inferior to God the Father and God the Son. This erroneous impression may have arisen mainly from the fact that the Holy Ghost is sent to the world by the Father and the Son, and has been manifested under the humble symbols of a dove and of tongues of fire. Now in order to ward off the danger to the purity and integrity of our faith involved in such a frame of mind, the Church gives us wonderful precisions as to the absolute and all-round equality of the Holy Spirit with both the Father and the Son.

Thus in the Nicene Creed we are made to profess:

"I believe in the Holy Ghost ... Who proceedeth from the Father and the Son: who, with the Father and the Son together is adored and glorified."

And in the Athanasian Creed:

"The Holy Spirit is from the Father and the Son—not made, nor created, nor begotten, but proceeding.... In this Trinity nothing is before or after, nothing greater or smaller, but all the three Persons are co-eternal and co-equal to each other."

This is so true, that we may, to some

extent and with due qualification, apply to the Holy Ghost also what St. John tells us of the Word, in the first verses of his Gospel. Thus we shall obtain the following statements:

"*In the beginning* was the Holy Spirit,

"And the Holy Spirit *was with God*,

"And the Holy Spirit *was God*.

"*The same was in the beginning with God* the Father and God the Son.

"*All things were made by Him, and without Him was made nothing that was made.*"

Thus far, but no farther, as it is obvious, can we literally apply the first verses of the Gospel of St. John both to the second and to the third Divine Persons. The Holy Ghost is God as fully as the other two Persons, from whom He proceeds in a manner which has no parallel among things created.

Now what is the Holy Ghost in Himself? In what relation does He stand to the other two Divine Persons? What is it that differentiates Him from them and makes Him to be what He is?

It is this:

THE BURNING BUSH

The Holy Ghost is the substantial, everlasting, infinite sweetness, emanating from the Father and the Son in their mutual embrace of love. Just as God the Son is the splendour of the Divine Essence, so is God the Holy Ghost the sweetness of the Divine Essence.

The inspired writer of the Book of Wisdom exclaims: *O how good and sweet is Thy spirit, O Lord!* (Wisd. xii, 1)—and in Ecclesiasticus, Divine Wisdom, the second Person of the Blessed Trinity, is introduced speaking in these terms: *I am the mother of fair love and of fear, and of knowledge, and of holy hope. In Me is all grace of the way and of the truth, in Me is all hope of life and of virtue. Come over to Me all ye that desire, and be filled with My fruits, for My spirit is sweet above honey* (Eccli. xxiv, 24-27).

This, then, is the description of the Holy Spirit, which the devout Christian, the mystic, will retain: the Holy Ghost is the substantial, everlasting sweetness of the Divine Essence as emanating from the Father and the Son; the Holy Ghost is THE VERY SWEETNESS OF GOD.

WONDERS OF THE THIRD PERSON

This peculiar and proper characteristic of the Holy Ghost, that of being the substantial sweetness of the Divine Essence as it proceeds from both the Father and the Son, is borne out by the copious testimony which Our Lord in His discourse at the Last Supper gave to His Apostles. A spiritual sweetness absolutely transcending all experiences of sensitive life, an illuminating and invigorating sweetness whose function in regard to men will be to minister to them consolation and keep them united in the love of Jesus.

If you love Me, says Our Lord, *keep My commandments, and I will ask the Father and He shall give you another Paraclete, that He may abide with you for ever, the Spirit of Truth whom the world cannot receive, because it seeth Him not, nor knoweth Him. But you shall know Him, because He shall abide with you and shall be in you* (John xiv, 15-17).

These things have I spoken to you, abiding with you, but the Paraclete, the Holy Ghost, whom the Father will send in My Name, He will teach you all things, and bring all things to your mind, whatso-

ever I shall have said to you (John xiv, 25-26).

When the Paraclete cometh, whom I will send you from the Father, the Spirit of Truth, who proceedeth from the Father, He will give testimony of Me (John xv, 26-27).

I tell you the truth: it is expedient for you that I go; for if I go not, the Paraclete will not come to you; but if I go, I shall send Him to you; and when He is come, He will convince the world of sin and of justice and of judgement (John xvi, 7, 8).

I have yet many things to say to you, but you cannot bear them now; but when He, the Spirit of Truth is come, He will teach you all truth; for He shall not speak of Himself; but what things soever He shall hear He shall speak; and the things that are to come He shall show you. He shall glorify Me, because He shall receive of Mine, and shall show it to you (John xvi, 12-14).

Just before His Ascension into heaven, Our Lord, eating with His Apostles, *commanded them that they should not depart from Jerusalem, but should wait for the promise of the Father, which you have heard (saith He) by my mouth. . . .*

You shall receive the power of the Holy Ghost coming upon you (Acts i, 4, 8).

O Holy Ghost, Sweetness of God and my very God, Thou art the substantial Breath of the Father and of the Son. Thou art Their infinite Sigh of contentment in each other's eternal embrace. Thou art Their Joy!

I adore Thee in Thyself.

And I adore Thee in Them both.

And I adore Thee in each of Them, distinct from both and one with Them: one and the same God!

The Holy Ghost is the only one of the three Divine Persons who does not produce another.

Shall we then conclude that He has no fecundity of His own? Far from this being the case, it is He who produces *ad extra* all those other persons who are divine, not, of course, by nature and essentially, but by communication of supernatural grace.

THE BURNING BUSH

It is the Holy Ghost who produced that masterpiece of Divine grace, the Immaculate Virgin Mary. It is the Holy Ghost who formed in her and of her virgin flesh, the human body of the Son of God at the same time as He created the human soul of the same and united it hypostatically to the Divine Word. To the Holy Ghost likewise must be attributed the production *in esse gratiae* of each one of the blessed children of God, either angels or men, and the gradual formation of the Church, the true Spouse of Christ.

These operations are the proper work of the Holy Spirit and demonstrate His wonderful fecundity which He holds from the Father and the Son. It is through the operation of the Holy Ghost that the diffusivity of the Sovereign Good which God is in Himself is made manifest.

My soul! Let us now try and see in what relation we stand in regard to the Holy Ghost.

Just as the Holy Spirit is the bond of union between the Father and the Son, so also is He the bond of union between both the Father and the Son and my puny self.

It is through Him that the Father loves the Son, and that reciprocally the Son loves the Father; and it is through Him that I am loved of both the Father and the Son and that I love Them in return.

I am dearly loved of the Father and of the Son: to be so loved what is it but to receive Their Holy Spirit? And, on the other hand, could I in any way return Them love for love but through the help of the Holy Ghost?

Let us even go down a little deeper in this consideration.

Between God the Father and God the Son everything begins with love and ends with love: is it not even so with me? Between God and me, everything begins in love. God has loved me first. God has loved me before He made me, and He made me precisely because He loved me. He loved me as God alone could love, that is to say from all eternity, with a view to all eternity; all the charities of my God towards me have followed hence. It is the substantial love of God, the Holy Ghost who brought me out of the depths of pure nothingness, where but for Him I would have slept for ever.

How rightly then is the Holy Spirit called a Gift, the great Gift, the first Gift! He is the Gift which the Father and the Son eternally bestow upon one another, and oh! how wonderful it is to think of it —He is the first Gift which the Father and the Son bestow upon the reasonable creature, upon me, even me, puny me!

My God, before such marvels I am struck dumb. Love is the only word. Love, love, love. Nothing but love!

CHAPTER XIV

THE BLESSED THREE IN ONE

SUMMARY.—A felicitous dogmatic formula. How the three Divine Persons are supremely One. Various images. A mystery it will remain for ever. Unicity of the Divine Essence and three diverse ways of possessing it. In each Person the mystery stands revealed. *Actus Purus* three times over.

AFTER all we have said thus far, it will readily be granted that in the work of contemplating the Most Holy Trinity it is not a question of our trying to understand this, the very greatest of all mysteries, as high above all the other mysteries proposed to our faith as heaven is above the earth. It is only a question—as we have already stated in a previous chapter—of our apprehending rightly the terms in which the mystery is proposed to our belief, so that we may render our acts of faith in it more real, and thus stir up in our hearts the flame of Divine Love.

In the Second Epistle of St. John we read:

THE BURNING BUSH

There are three who give testimony in heaven: the Father, the Word, and the Holy Ghost, and these three are One.

Some modern exegetists have tried to make out that those words are an interpolation in the sacred text. Even if this were proved to be the case—which is far from being established upon any evidence that is convincing—the fact of the Church having made them quite her own by inserting them in the sacred liturgy would suffice to confer upon them the dignity of a dogmatic utterance. And, indeed, the mystery of the Blessed Trinity could hardly be set forth in a more felicitous formula: *There are three who give testimony in heaven: the Father, the Word, and the Holy Ghost, and these three are One:* three Persons and one only God.

We must not represent to ourselves the three Divine Persons as we would for instance a group of three angels; for three angels have each one a different nature from the other two. Nor as we would a group of three men, for though they have the same human nature, yet each one of them possesses it so individualized

THE BLESSED THREE IN ONE

in himself that he stands as a separate, complete substance by himself, with an independent life all his own; whilst the three Divine Persons have together one and the same nature, they are together one and the same substance, one and the same *Actus Purus*, the Supreme Being, supremely One.

Three men holding together their arms lovingly entwined behind each other's necks are for the time being as though they were knit together: one of them cannot take a step but that the other two go with him; and they may very well be but one in heart; still for all that, they have, even then, each his own separate life, and, of course, they cannot remain thus locked together in such a tight embrace, they will have eventually to separate. Not so the three Divine Persons, because the three together are one only, indivisible, incorruptible Divine Essence.

Once I was shown a very surprising piece of workmanship: an ivory ball, or rather shell, of the size of an orange, pierced with a network of holes which permitted one to see within it a second ball or shell, likewise perforated in the same way, and within the second one also a third. Might this serve as a material image of the manner in which the three Divine Persons are one only God, and within each other? No: for the first ball contains the other two, but is not contained within them; the second contains within itself the third one, but not the first; and the third does not contain either of the other two. Moreover, these three balls are not equal but of gradually diminishing size; whilst the three Divine Persons are so enclosed within one another that each contains within itself the other two, and the three are absolutely equal in all things, possessing each the same infinite perfections.

Says the Athanasian Creed:

"Such as the Father, such is the Son, such is the Holy Spirit. The Father is uncreated: uncreated also is the Son, uncreated the Holy Spirit. The Father is immense; equally immense is the Son, immense the Holy Spirit. The Father is eternal: eternal is the Son, eternal is the Holy Spirit. The Father is God: God is the Son, God is the Holy Spirit, and yet not three Gods but one only God."

THE BLESSED THREE IN ONE

Contrasted with the example of the three ivory balls all in one, the popular comparison of the sprig of shamrock, due to St. Patrick, to help rude minds to give their assent to the fundamental mystery of our faith, is a much more felicitous one, though failing in part, as all comparisons cannot but do. At least the three leaves of the sprig of shamrock are equal to each other and stand all three on one and the same stem. That this cannot serve to illustrate the mutual inhabitation of each of the three Divine Persons in the other two is obvious.

When all has been said or tried, we are compelled to confess that this is a mystery and the greatest of all mysteries. We apprehend the terms in which it is expressed, and we believe it upon God's very own testimony, therefore our assent to it is perfectly rational and fully justified; and, moreover, this assent of ours is in the highest degree supernatural and could not be yielded by us but with the help of Divine grace: but a mystery it remains. And though in glory we shall see God face to face, and witness His Divine life as it is *ad intra* and see the Divine operations of the eternal

THE BURNING BUSH

generation of the Son and the eternal breathing out of the Holy Ghost, a mystery it will remain for evermore to all the elect of God. The reason of this is that, although the created intellect may, by grace, or more expressly by the *lumen gloriae*, be raised above itself to the point of apprehending God in an immediate manner, yet it remains fundamentally and everlastingly incapable of grasping His fulness. Only God can fathom God or understand or express Him fully. However, let us hasten to add that it were wrong to fancy that the happiness of the Blessed will, on this score, suffer any curtailment.

On the contrary, this very fact of the absolute infinitude and incomprehensibleness of God will be to them a subject of joy and of praise, for ever fresh and inexhaustible. They would not have it otherwise, being well aware that a God whom they could comprehend would be no God at all.

The unity of God consists in the unicity of the Divine Essence; the Trinity of Persons is founded on the three diverse ways of possessing this one and the same

Divine Essence. The Father possesses it as of Himself, and communicates it to the Son by way of generation. The Son possesses it as received from the Father, and together with the Father He communicates it to the Holy Spirit. The Holy Spirit receives it from both the Father and the Son, united in one principle of active spiration, and does not communicate it to anyone soever, because in Him is completed the full cycle of the Divine life.

Therefore the Father is the Divine Essence uncommunicated; the Son is this same identical Divine Essence communicated from the first to the second Person; the Holy Ghost is that same identical Divine Essence as it is in common in the Father and the Son, communicated jointly from these two first Persons to a third one, by way of spiration.

Thus the three Divine Persons have one and the same Divine Essence, which is absolutely incommunicable to anyone else.

So that, to hold the fulness of the Divine Nature from no one but from oneself is to be God the Father; to hold the fulness of the Divine Nature as communicated from

THE BURNING BUSH

the Father alone is to be God the Son; finally, to hold the fulness of the Divine Nature from both together the Father and Son is to be the Holy Spirit.

The Father is the supreme, absolute, infinite Good; the Son is the Splendour of this supreme, absolute, infinite Good; the Holy Ghost is the Sweetness of this supreme, absolute, infinite Good. (We need hardly advert to the fact that here we use the word Good as a substantive noun, not as an adjective.)

In each of the Divine Persons the whole mystery of the Blessed Trinity stands revealed. I cannot view God the Father without being made aware that He has a Son and loves Him and is loved of Him infinitely, thereby producing the Holy Spirit. I cannot view the Divine Son without being made aware that He has a Father whom He loves and of whom He is loved infinitely and therefore also a Holy Ghost. I cannot view the Holy Spirit without being made aware of whom He is the Spirit—namely, of the Father and of the Son.

THE BLESSED THREE IN ONE

Although these three Divine Persons are consubstantial, and co-eternal and co-equal in all things, being one and the same Divine Nature, yet there is between them a natural and inviolable order, the Father being the first, the Son being the second, and the Holy Spirit being the third.

I am who am, says God to Moses, speaking to him from amidst the flames of the burning bush.

By these words God the Father describes the fulness of life with which He produces and carries in His bosom His Divine Word and the Holy Spirit of love. The Bush represents God the Father, the bright flame which shoots forth from it without separating itself from it, represents the Divine Word; and finally, the heat which emanates at the same time from the bush and the flame, aptly represents the Spirit of love.

Actus Purus, what is it again but God the Father who has never been a single instant without begetting His Divine Son, or without immediately producing with Him His Holy Spirit? Does perchance the fact of there being three distinct Divine Persons preclude the Divine Essence in

God the Father from being *Actus Purus?* Nay, it but serves to intensify, if one may say so, the pureness of that act which God the Father is. In reality God is *Actus Purus* three times over. God the Father, through God the Son, in the unity of God the Holy Ghost as He is revealed to us in the Catholic dogma, is such an *Actus Purus* as the sublimest among philosophers never could have risen to conceive.

The whole Divine life proceeds from God the Father to His Divine Son and returns to Him through Their Holy Spirit: proceeds from Him without going out of Him: returns to Him without having been separated from Him. He is a marvellous abysmal fountain which ever springs and ever flows within its own Divine Self.

Oh, let us adore in silence!

PART II—GOD IN HIS WORKS

CHAPTER XV

ON THE OPERATIONS OF GOD CALLED "AD EXTRA"

SUMMARY.—What is meant and also what is not meant by "operations *ad extra*." How numerous and varied. All summed up in the three: Creation, Redemption, Sanctification—appropriated respectively to the Father, the Son, and the Holy Ghost—and further summed up in the fulfilling of Jesus Christ.

IN Part I, just now concluded, we have proposed to the devout contemplation of the mystic, the Lord God in Himself, in His operations *ad intra*, as the theologians put it—that is to say, in those Divine operations which give rise to the Trinity of Persons in the unity of the Divine Essence.

We now proceed to the loving contemplation of God in His Works—that is to say, in the results of His operations *ad extra*.

We call operations *ad extra*, those Divine

operations whose terms are the things created.

Of course, this expression *ad extra* must not be taken as meaning that God causes anything whatever to exist independently of Himself, for, as the Apostle says: *In Him we live and move and are* (Acts xvii, 28). All things are necessarily in God and could not otherwise exist. Even sinners at the very time of their committing sin, even reprobate souls and fallen angels, even hell itself, along with the rest of things created, are in God and God is in them. God is in them necessarily, in virtue of His attribute of Immensity, and they are in God as their First Cause, whose creative energy sustains their being.

The operations of God *ad extra*, considered from our human point of view, are almost infinitely numerous and varied—as numerous, indeed, and varied as individual created objects and persons, past, present, and future, and their component parts, and their actions and reactions upon each other, and their mutual relations. For there is not, nor can there be, a single effect proceeding from a secondary cause, which does not constantly require a vital influx from the Primary Cause—that is to say, from God Himself.

Still, infinitely numerous and varied though they be, the operations of God *ad extra* may all be summed up in the three following:

1. Creation and providential government of the whole world of things, visible and invisible.

2. Incarnation of the Son of God and His Redemption of the fallen race of mankind.

3. Sanctification of the predestinate, during the present life under the regimen of faith, in the next world, through the unfolding of the state of glory.

Each one of those three wonderful operations of God *ad extra* is, for reasons of fitness, appropriated, that is to say, assigned particularly, to one of the Divine Persons: Creation to the Father, Redemption to the Son, Sanctification to the Holy Spirit—though each one of them is really, according to a well-known axiom of dogmatic theology, the joint work of the three Divine Persons.

THE BURNING BUSH

These three Divine operations sum up the whole activity of God as it is poured out of His own Divine life. Nay, even these three are all summed up in the one great work of God, which is the fulfilling of Our Lord Jesus Christ, *the Son of Man*, as He loved to call Himself, for, indeed, the Most Holy Trinity made all things in Him and for Him. The great work *ad extra* of the Blessed Trinity lies in the fulfilment of Our Lord Jesus Christ in time and throughout eternity.

All that this means we shall only know after the general resurrection of the dead and the Last Judgement.

CHAPTER XVI

ON THE PRETENDED PLURALITY OF WORLDS

SUMMARY.—Two attitudes possible in front of the universe. Not a scrap of scientific evidence in favour of the hypothesis of a plurality of independent closed systems of stars, or of planets being inhabited by other human races. Dogmatic revelation dead against the last supposition. We have a better plurality of worlds to consider.

IN front of the flaming hieroglyphics of the universe of things visible and invisible two attitudes are possible.

Bearing in mind that all those wonderful things are the work of God, a man may endeavour to find in them a certain revelation of Him and ever fresh incentives to love Him. That is the right attitude to take.

Or a man may choose, more or less deliberately and consciously, to look upon all this marvellous universe, simply with secularized eyes, not seeking God in it, nor caring to hearken to any supernal message which it may bear to us.

It is to such men that the wise and bitter Ecclesiastes alluded when he penned this sentence:

God hath made all things good in their time, and hath delivered the world to their consideration, so that man cannot find out the work which God hath made from the beginning to the end (Eccles. iii, 11).

People talk glibly of a certain plurality of worlds, by them supposed as probable. Some mean thereby to convey the idea that in the starry world at large or even nearer home to us in some planets of our own solar system, there be lands inhabited by other human races different from our own. Others go still further and would have us believe that far away from our visible universe there exist many conglomerations of stars comparable to our nebula of the Milky Way, but separated from it and from each other, forming each a closed system, perfectly independent and autonomous—a world by itself.

Such fanciful hypotheses may serve to

PLURALITY OF WORLDS

amuse people endowed with more imagination than sound judgement, but the truth must be told that not an atom of scientific evidence can be produced in favour of these contentions.

As far as the pretended stellar systems, independent of our own, are concerned, we must note two things: either these new worlds are by us discoverable or they are not.

If they be not, how can one ever talk of them? To reason about their existence at all is a futile and first-rate absurdity. Only a mountebank bent upon feeding the gullibility of an ignorant and stupid audience of villagers can have the brazen effrontery to hold forth in the name of science on such a topic.

On the other hand, if these pretended new worlds are by us discoverable, it must be by some direct, experimental process; but this would at once do away with the contention that those starry conglomerations form so many separate and independent closed systems, in no way related to our own. For in order to be discoverable by us, they must, of necessity, have a relation of distance and co-ordination and harmony with our own world, and thereby form one universe with it.

It is clear that such wild speculations can in no way contribute to the furtherance of our knowledge of the real state of things in the universe, still less of our knowledge of the good and loving God; rather the reverse. All they are good for is to puff us up with insane pride and feed our hungry souls with wind.

As for other races of men living, either on the planet Mars or on any other sphere of this vast universe, not only is there not the slightest evidence in favour of such a supposition, but the whole weight of the dogmatic teaching of the Divine revelation goes dead against it. True, neither the Bible nor the Church make any pronouncement expressly against this hypothesis: they simply ignore it. But it does look indeed as if what they do tell us authoritatively, of the manner and scope and limits of creation, could in no way be reconciled with such a plurality of human races. One has only to read attentively and with an open mind the first chapter of Genesis in

PLURALITY OF WORLDS

order to see that the hypothesis of other human races besides our own is as inadmissible as that of other closed systems of worlds.

Then the mystery of the Incarnation and what Our Lord tells us of the Kingdom of Heaven, present and yet to come, and of the Last Judgement and of the regeneration of the whole universe when He will make all things new—all this, I say, seems absolutely to foreclose the idea of any other human race being actually in existence besides our own: though it must be conceded that God could, if He saw fit, create such other races. The question is not one of what is possible, but of what is actually a demonstrable fact.

Let us put away all these childish imaginations.

Whilst silly people pursue a shadow they lose the substance. We shall be better advised, if we make use first of all of what we know for certain.

Thereby we shall find so rich, so delightful, so inexhaustible a fountain of knowledge, so marvellous an object of contemplation, so full of God and making us love

Him, that we shall have no use for the above-mentioned idle speculations.

We have, indeed, a better plurality of worlds, and immensely more interesting, if only we will attend to it, worlds within worlds, a hierarchy of worlds, admirably co-ordinated, throwing light one upon the other and leading us up to a wonderful increase of knowledge of the good and loving God who made them.

This we now proceed to consider.

CHAPTER XVII

The Greatest World under the Blessed Trinity

SUMMARY.—The greatest world under the Blessed Trinity, the Human Soul of Our Lord Jesus Christ. Infinitude of grace and power it derives from the hypostatic union. Divine diffusiveness. The Divine plan. Order of the Divine emanations.

THE greatest of all worlds—this goes without saying—is the Divine Essence, in the uncreated infinite, ineffable Trinity of its Persons, a world which even eternity will not suffice to enable the blessed Angels and men fully to explore; a world compared with which all others, rolled into one, are but a faint shadow.

Next to the Blessed Trinity, the very first and greatest of all worlds is, not this conglomeration of bright spheres which we call our visible universe, nor the dazzling hierarchy of the nine choirs of the blessed angels in glory, but this mightiest and most ineffable of the works of God, the Human Soul of Our Lord Jesus Christ.

In Our Lord two natures are united in one Person: the Divine Nature of the Son of God, and a human soul and body which derive from their hypostatic union with the Word of God an infinitude of grace, and dignity, and power and resources which baffle all understanding.

Our Lord is the first and last word of Creation, the *Alpha and Omega* of it, as He calls Himself in the Apocalypse (i, 8), the reason of it all, the explanation of all.

Let us try and consider this a little more closely.

The very first feature of God, which His works reveal to us, is His diffusiveness, or that perfection of His in virtue of which He loves to communicate Himself and share His own goods with others.

Even pagan philosophers were aware that "bonum est sui diffusivum," and that God, being supremely good, is therefore supremely inclined to spread abroad and communicate to others some emanations of His.

But as these philosophers were ignorant

THE GREATEST WORLD

of the supernatural revelation, they missed much of what it is now our privilege to contemplate. They could never suspect how greatly this infinite fire of love, which God is, wants to manifest itself to us in the burning bush or forest of things created, not consuming them, but speaking to us from their midst, and thereby imparting to us even now, and in proportion as we let Him, a share of His own Divine sanctity and happiness.

It was with this end in view that God resolved to create reasonable beings, angels and men, in His own image and likeness, and to raise them, even from the beginning, to a state of grace absolutely above their natural requirements and out of their natural reach.

And now we come to the nucleus of the question, to the core and heart of the subject of this chapter, for in order to carry out His benevolent intentions God decreed, first of all, that His Son, the second Person of the Holy Trinity, should in the fulness of time become man, and that all things should be put under His dominion, that He might bring them all back to God Who made them, that all things might be in Him, with Him, and through Him sanctified, and give glory to the Blessed Trinity: angels from the beginning, men through the succeeding ages. Church history, nay, the history of the whole world is simply the unfolding of this Divine plan.

Obviously, the hypostatic union with which the human soul and body of Our Lord are favoured is a created grace. It is not an essential, necessary, and eternal union like that which exists between the three Divine Persons. It is the union of a created thing—namely, the Sacred Humanity, with the Person of the Word: a union which is not required by the Divine Nature of the Word, nor by the human nature of the body and soul of Christ, but which is wholly the work of the Divine pleasure of the Blessed Trinity. But it is really the most marvellous work of God, the one which best reveals, by reflecting them, His infinite perfections.

The human soul of Christ is a marvellous mirror of the power, wisdom, and sweetness of the three Divine Persons. In its quasi-infinite amplitude it is a world, a mighty

THE GREATEST WORLD

world, the depth and height and length and breadth of which no created intellect, either human or angelical, will ever be able to fathom. By the grace of the hypostatic union, it extends beyond all limits and is able to afford shelter not only to all men of goodwill, but as well to all the blessed angelic natures. We are all in Christ Jesus. We all receive from His fulness. By grace we are made one with Him. The ivory sphere containing yet others, which we have introduced in a previous chapter, might perhaps serve as an apt illustration of the all-embracing capacity of the human Soul of Our Lord Jesus Christ.

Now we may proceed to set down the order of the Divine emanations on things created.

Roughly speaking it is as follows:

1. The fulness of natural perfection and of Divine grace has been poured upon the Sacred Humanity of Our Lord Jesus Christ.

2. Under Christ, the Head, and in Him and through Him, there has taken place a measureless outpouring of Divine grace upon the Church of the predestinate whilst

THE BURNING BUSH

still actually in the making, and which will ultimately consist of the blessed Angels and all the Saints.

3. And first of all, and in an absolutely transcending proportion, there has been made a pouring out of the grace of God through Jesus Christ, upon the first and principal member of His Church—namely, the Virgin Mary, His Immaculate Mother, Queen of Heaven, of all Saints, and of all creation.

4. Then, out of the fulness of grace of Jesus and Mary, the emanations of God, poured forth upon the nine choirs of the blessed Angels, descending as a marvellous waterfall from the highest through all the intervening degrees, even to the lowest.

5. Then again, out of the same fulness of the grace of Jesus and Mary, and enlisting the ministrations of the blessed Angels, the Divine emanations spread upon all the Saints that have been made up to this present moment, wherever they be, in the bliss of Paradise, in Purgatory, or here on earth.

6. Then also the Divine emanations on the poor sinners.

For, indeed, whatever of natural goodness still subsists in them is evidently a certain emanation of the very goodness of God and is imparted to them through Jesus Christ.

Thus far we have only spoken of the emanations of God which result in the goodness both natural and supernatural of the reasonable creatures. Now we must mention:

7. The emanations of God upon the whole world of inferior creatures, conferring upon all and each the goodness of some far resemblance to Him, *quasi per vestigia*, say the theologians, "as through His footprints" or the impress of His creative hands, faintly delineating and in various ways expressing His infinite perfections.

8. Finally, there is even in the fallen angels and reprobate men, as well as in all the other creatures, high or low, animate or inanimate, the emanation of the essential, transcendental goodness of God, by which, as philosophers express it, *ens et bonum* are said to be convertible terms. This means that all that God made, all that actually is, in so far as it is, is good.

Evil is not a positive entity, but only a privation.

There is no substantial evil of any kind. Evil is always, in every case, the absence of some quality or perfection which the nature or circumstances of the subject require. In the reasonable creatures—angels or men—evil results from the guilty acts by which they freely put aside the above described supernatural emanations and wrench themselves from the loving grasp of the Sacred Humanity of Our Lord Jesus Christ.

O my God, Most Holy Trinity, how wonderful art Thou in all the works of Thy blessed hands, but most of all in the greatest, which is the Sacred Humanity of Our Lord Jesus Christ. In Him and with Him and through Him, be Thou blessed for ever!

CHAPTER XVIII

THE NEXT GREATEST CREATED WORLD, THE BLESSED VIRGIN MARY

SUMMARY.—The only created world, after Jesus Christ, in which God has not suffered disappointment. The great things God has done to Mary. How we must understand that she is full of grace. A revelation of God's loving kindness and mercy. The universal Mother. The pedestal of the Golden Candlestick.

THE second greatest created world, situate immediately below the Sacred Humanity of Our Blessed Lord, is the marvellous one formed by the Person of the ever Blessed Virgin Mary, with her immaculate body and soul, in their wonderful relations to each of the three Divine Persons and to all the angels and men and to the inferior material universe.

Mary is, of all pure creatures, the one nearest to God, most like to Him, the one who received most from Him and who renders to Him the greatest glory.

Together with the Sacred Humanity of

THE BURNING BUSH

Our Lord, with which she is so intimately connected and from which she receives all her reflected bright light, even as the moon takes its own from the sun, Mary is the only created world in which God has not suffered some disappointment; for, on the one hand, Our Lord being God and man cannot be ranged among the pure creatures, and, on the other hand, the worlds inferior to Mary, as we shall soon see, have each failed, as a whole, to correspond to the will of God in their behalf.

Mary is, after Our Lord Jesus Christ, the most splendid revelation of God. She herself proclaims in her Magnificat: *He that is mighty hath done great things to me.* No mistake about this; Mary stands as the greatest manifestation of how far the power of God extends in the making of a pure creature like unto Him. This may be put in relief by a few questions. Thus:

Can Divine Omnipotence, out of the whole *massa perdita* of a fallen race, preserve incorrupt and save beforehand, by a higher redemption, one single member to be used for the purpose of the future redemption of the others? Mary is the reply.

THE NEXT GREATEST WORLD

Can Divine Omnipotence render a human creature not only immaculate in her conception, but, moreover, without the least interfering with the free play of her will, impeccable? Mary is the reply.

Can Divine Omnipotence raise a pure creature to the very confines or borderland, so to say, of the Godhead, *usque ad fines divinitatis* (to use a forcible and felicitous expression of Suarez); so that she should become the true and natural mother of God, and bring forth in her virgin flesh the Eternal Word of God? Mary is the reply.

Can Divine Omnipotence form a human heart so deep and so strong as to contain, on the one hand, more sorrow at some time of her earthly life than has ever been experienced by all angels and men *in viâ;* and, on the other hand, more joy—at least after her admission to the Beatific Vision—than will ever be imparted to all angels and saints together? Mary is the reply. For, indeed, Mary's joys over her Divine motherhood for ever will be as deep and sublime as heaven itself; and her compassion and sorrow over the passion and death of her Divine Son have been as vast as the ocean, says the prophet Jeremias (Thren. ii, 13).

Truly *He that is mighty hath done great things* to her.

The ambassador-angel, speaking in the name of his Master the Tri-une God, proclaimed her "full of grace."

In order that we should realize the significance of this praise, we must bear in mind what a wonderful capacity God has given her. The blessed Angels are all full of grace, so are all the Saints in Paradise, nay, even sometimes whilst still here on earth; but Mary has the capacity of the ocean.

Compared to her the blessed Angels and all the Saints are as so many vessels of all sizes deposited on the sea-shore, which are all filled from its very fulness without causing any appreciable diminution of the same. True, the ocean itself has its limits, and so has the grace of the Blessed Virgin Mary, but those limits can be known but of God.

More than anything else, Mary is to us a revelation of the most touching attribute of the Divine Essence, its goodness, or, in other terms, its loving-kindness, and in Mary this revelation is brought within the grasp of our limited capacity.

God in Himself is far too much above us, too dazzling for our puny understanding, but now behold Mary, a creature even like ourselves—a woman—the Virgin Mother of His Son, bearing Him a little child in her arms, and presenting Him to the loving adoration of the world: Can anything more sweet be imagined? Could any more touching demonstration of the loving-kindness of God be invented?

And, above all, Mary expresses and puts in strong relief this peculiar aspect of the goodness, of the loving-kindness of God, the Divine Mercy. It is not for nothing that her heart has been created so deep and wide: it was to embrace in her motherly love, together with her Divine Son, all that are Christ's, both angels and men. More than the first Eve, Mary is the universal Mother, and bears a personal, providential relation not only to each of the redeemed of her Divine Son, but also to each of the blessed pure spirits. This we shall see clearly when we come to heaven. Meanwhile, we believe it and praise the Divine Goodness for it.

She is the created pedestal of the Godhead.

Upon that pedestal stands that seven-branched golden candlestick, the Light of the world, Our Lord, from whom the nine choirs of angels and all the orders of the Saints receive their illumination, in time and throughout all eternity.

Only two virgins ever bore a son—namely, first and from all eternity God the Father; and then, in time, Mary. Thus is Mary a certain revelation of God the Father, and of the Virginal Fecundity that characterizes Him.

The Apostles have duly celebrated the immensity of the grace of Mary when they wrote in the Creed:

"I believe in God the Father . . . and in Jesus Christ His only Son . . . Who WAS BORN OF THE VIRGIN MARY."

O my God, Most Holy Trinity, how admirable art Thou in that masterpiece of

THE NEXT GREATEST WORLD

Thy creative hands, the ever Blessed Virgin, the unique Daughter of Thee, O God the Father, the incomparable Mother of Thee, O God the Son, the spotless Spouse of Thee, O Holy Spirit! Be Thou, O most Holy Trinity, blessed in her for evermore!

CHAPTER XIX

The Third Greatest Created World

SUMMARY.—The Church of the Predestinate. Of what elements it is made up. God has suffered some disappointment: first in angels, then in the human race. Each predestinate is a little world within the greater one. Each single angel, a whole nature. The first Church Militant. That God reveals Himself in the Saints. Their wonderful personality. Many vessels of gold, adorned with every precious stone. Their various orders.

THE third greatest created world is the Church of the Predestinate. Still in the making as it is, it nevertheless reveals already the glory of the Blessed Trinity—the power, the wisdom, and the goodness of God—to a marvellous extent.

It is made up of the following elements: first, all the blessed angelic natures, then all the departed souls of men who are already in heaven or in purgatory, and, finally, all the men of goodwill on earth.

The Church of the Predestinate was prefigured in the mysterious chariot of which both the prophet Ezechiel, in his first chapter, and St. John the Evangelist, in chapters iv and v of his Apocalypse, give us a description, and which Ezechiel calls *the vision of the likeness of the glory of God* (Ezech. ii, 1). It already has a wonderful history in the past ages, and, furthermore, the promises of eternal life, that life of which we sing in the Nicene Creed: *Credo . . . vitam venturi saeculi.*

True, it must be owned that God has suffered some disappointment—to express it in a human way—first of all in the angels, a third part of whom fell away from grace, and then in the human race as a whole, since Adam and Eve fell away from their state of innocence and we all fell away in them (the Blessed Virgin Mary alone excepted), and since even after the Redemption of the Cross, so many men will not be saved. But this only serves the more to show to us what a wonderful work of God is the Church of the Predestinate; hewn out, so to say, stone by stone, from these two great quarries, the angelic world as God created it in the beginning, and the whole human race as God is creating it through succeeding centuries.

THE BURNING BUSH

Each of the blessed Angels and each of the Saints, whether already glorified or not, is in himself a revelation of God, a little world within the greater world of the full assembly of them.

A little world which gives to God particular glory, and which adds to the splendour of the whole; a touch, as it were, of colour and a distinct note in the melody, which could not be dispensed with. It is a wheel within a wheel of the mysterious chariot *of the vision of the likeness of the glory of God—rota in medio rotae*—a fixed star out of the dazzling galaxy of the nine angelic choirs and the various orders of the Saints. But what a multitude of them! and how therein also shines the power and the beauty and the love of the Most Holy Trinity who made them!

To speak first of the blessed Angels in particular.

Each of them is a pure spiritual nature, made in the image of God, intelligent and free, simple, incorruptible, inexterminable; raised by grace to the supernatural state, from which not only he never fell away, but did not waver a single instant; destined from the first to eternal glory. He was put upon his trial together with all the other angels, he bravely fought and conquered and was immediately crowned, and is now gloriously employed in active service for the formation of the Church of the Predestinate, as it is to be after the end of the world.

Each of the angels is a whole nature, different from all the others, a world in himself, in which the attributes and perfections of the Blessed Trinity reflect themselves and shine forth with an exclusive lustre, peculiar to that angel. They are all related to one another and co-ordinated into various choirs of dazzling cumulative beauty. They are most noble children of the heavenly Father; willing, whole-hearted servants of the Incarnation, and our own loving elder brothers. Before we came upon this planet of ours they were the first Church Militant, and though their trial was swift, it was keenly searching.

With inexpressible spiritual sadness, they witnessed the defection and fall of those who were their well-beloved brethren, who in their very midst suddenly turned traitors to God, enemies of themselves, tempters of their brethren, in one word devils, and became monstrously malicious and ugly. Under the leadership of Michael, the faithful angels stood the brunt of the battle. With their eyes fixed on God, they bravely fought for justice and truth, without any respect of persons, without false commiseration or unworthy bargaining. They came out of this terrible ordeal, having preserved absolutely unsullied their first sanctity, infused in them at the moment of their creation: nay, it was then and there, by the very act, prodigiously increased, and at once blossomed out into the glory of the Beatific Vision. This much about the blessed Angels in glory.

And now about the Saints, those other living stones of the heavenly Jerusalem that is in the making. By Saints I mean all men of goodwill, wheresoever they be, in heaven or in purgatory or here on earth. But in regard to those on earth I mean particularly Christians who have passed the first two stages of the spiritual life and are arrived at the Way of Union. They are

THE THIRD GREATEST WORLD

the perfect ones, the heroes of the spiritual life, the ideal Christians.

Now in all these, wherever they be, God reveals Himself, shining forth through their body and soul. God manifests His power, wisdom, and love in each of them, in an original, unique manner according to each one's peculiar character, so that we can truly say of each of them: *There was not found the like of him: Non est inventus similis illi* (Eccli. xliv, 20).

The Saints are, of all men, the only ones who develop their own personality to the highest degree. Other people servilely copy or plagiarize each other. As for those young and giddy ones who behave outrageously and give as an excuse that they want to live their own lives and are seeking to realize themselves, be it known that they are duping and deluding themselves egregiously. Only the Saints live their own lives and realize themselves, and they do it thoroughly, splendidly, magnificently. And they do it almost unknown to themselves: their only care being to root out of themselves all disordered affections and to allow God to have His own way with them in everything. But the result is marvellous.

The inspired writer of Ecclesiasticus has penned six wonderful chapters in praise of the holy men of old, which I wish I could insert bodily here, were it not for their great length. They are chapters xliv to l inclusively. I ask my reader to look them up for himself in his Bible and ponder over them at leisure. I will cull out of them only one verse. In chapter l, verse 11, it is said of Simon the high priest that he was *as a massy vessel of gold, adorned with every precious stone.* Now this applies as well to each one of the dear Saints of God wherever found, but to each with a difference.

Let us represent to ourselves an immense number of vessels of purest gold, in an infinite variety of forms and sizes, every one chiselled differently.

Each is adorned with the large carbuncles of Faith, Hope, and Charity, and with the four gems of Prudence, Justice, Temperance, and Fortitude, and with the countless precious pearls and diamonds of their own personal merits. The rim of every vessel is outwardly hung round with seven rings or handles of a metal more precious than gold, I mean the seven gifts of the Holy Spirit, inserted in the soul through the sacraments, and ready to the hand of God to lift up the vessel and raise it to any height of heroic sanctity, as soon as it has been emptied of all created affections and has filled itself with God, God, God alone.

I say, represent to yourselves an immense number and variety of such vessels in heaven, in the fiery furnace of Purgatory and here on earth, scattered through the length and breadth of the Church Militant. Now, will not such a magnificent display of the handicraft of the three Divine Persons help us to conceive an exalted idea of Him who made them for His glory? And will it not move us to praise Him and to love Him?

The bare enumeration of the various orders of Saints ought to throw us into raptures, if we will only think over the perfections of God which they reflect and reveal. Innocents, virgins, confessors, penitents, pontiffs, martyrs, patriarchs, prophets, doctors, apostles, and apostolic men. Truly *God is admirable in His saints* (Ps. lxvii, 36).

Join all these to the nine choirs of the blessed Angels, and you have the Church of the Predestinate as it is now, and you obtain a glimpse of what is, indeed, a most marvellous work of the Blessed Trinity.

It takes this great multitude of angels and saints, and those that will in the future be added to their number, somehow to express the sanctity of Our Lord Jesus Christ.

They are the garden of God, where the three Divine Persons take their delight.

They are the sea of glass before the throne of the Divine Majesty, which receives and reflects faithfully the image of the ineffable sanctity of the Blessed Trinity.

They are the living lyres vibrating under the fingers and breath of the Holy Spirit, to form the grand concert of the perfect praise of God.

O my God, Most Holy Trinity, Father, Son, and Holy Ghost, be Thou blessed for ever in this magnificent work of Thine, the Church of the Predestinate!

CHAPTER XX

THE WORLD OF MATTER, FROM STARS TO ATOMS

SUMMARY.—It is the humblest in the scale of worlds as we are considering them, and still very stupendous. The untutored Arab *versus* the European atheist. A starlit night. The atom of hydrogen. The composition of matter, of ether. Man's mind superior to the world of matter. Creation a thin veil on the radiant face of God.

IN the scale of worlds as we are considering them by means of the joint light of reason and revelation, and as so many mirrors which reflect the glory of the Blessed Trinity, the humblest, the least, and yet, indeed, a magnificent work of God, is this material universe of ours: this stellar world of which our solar system is but a very tiny component, whilst our sphere, the earth, seems to be all but lost in its immensity, as a pebble on the seashore, as a speck in a sunbeam, as an atom, comparatively speaking.

THE BURNING BUSH

A very beautiful world!

The Church does not hesitate to sing in the *Te Deum: O thrice Holy Lord, God of Hosts, full are the heavens and the earth of the majesty of Thy glory.*

Full with the praise of the glory of the majesty of God: yes, so they are, but only for those who have ears to hear and eyes to see.

This stupendous concave, as it seems to us, of the blue firmament overhead, with its myriads of stars and simply inconceivable stellar spaces, which so wrought upon mad Pascal's sensibilities, let us but fill it with the sweet presence of the loving God, and we shall derive from its contemplation an overwhelming torrent of joy.

Here is the *Pensée* of the celebrated man of genius with a strain of melancholy and a touch of Jansenism: "*Le silence éternel de ces espaces infinis m'effraye*" (The eternal silence of those infinite spaces affrights me).

But they are not silent, and he ought to have known it; they speak, they sing, they shout.

From the dawn of creation they sound forth in an unbroken melody, the praise of

THE WORLD OF MATTER

the Most Holy Tri-une God who made them.

> *The heavens show forth the glory of God,*
> *And the firmament declareth the work of His hands.*
> *Day to day uttereth speech,*
> *And night to night showeth knowledge.*
> *There are no speeches nor languages,*
> *Where their voices are not heard.*
> Ps. xviii.

The untutored Arab of the desert, the savages of both Americas and of Australia, all hear and understand. It takes a sophisticated and effete civilization as that of Europe nowadays to produce this monstrosity, an atheist, upon whose sensibilities and intelligence the appeal of the firmament by day and night falls in vain.

The most magnificent and entrancing spectacle set before our eyes is, without any doubt, that of a starlit night, especially in those regions where the atmosphere is purest, as for instance in the Sahara Desert. It is far more entrancing and beautiful than the dazzling splendours of midday or the wonderful display of colours of any dawn or sunset, because more mysterious, more awe-inspiring, more heavily freighted with a Divine message.

The splendours of early dawn, or midday, or sunset are, after all, but the illumination of a tiny corner of our solar system, whilst a starlit night seems to open before us a vista of infinitude itself.

And it is not only in its prodigious extent, the dimensions of which we utterly fail to realize, but as well in its every detail, down to the smallest, such as an insect, a blade of grass, a dewdrop, a grain of sand, an atom, that the universe bears the impress of God, the seal of the Most Holy Trinity, showing forth infinite power, infinite wisdom, and infinite sweetness. These tiny objects, each and all, show forth the omnipotence of God. Each of them is a Divine idea realized in a concrete form, a small world in itself; a surprising complex of laws and of actions and reactions; a closed system: in a word, an abyss wherein man's reason loses itself hopelessly.

Take, for instance, an atom of hydrogen.

THE WORLD OF MATTER

It is the most common and best known of all so far. By the complexity of its structure, the intensity of its life, the prodigious swiftness of the movements of its component electrons around a central nucleus, it is, upon an infinitesimally small scale, the very counterpart of any of the solar systems which fill the depths of the firmament.

By methods of observation which it would require a whole volume to explain to the uninitiated, it has been ascertained that in this, the simplest of all atoms, each of the particles which surround its central nucleus performs no less than five million oscillating movements in a second. But that is a comparatively modest number. The atoms of other so-called simple elements show an immense increase of swiftness of movements, and we are yet but on the threshold of the new world of wonders which the discovery of radium and other such substances have of late been opening before us.

From this it will be seen that we are very far, indeed, from having reached the final word on the question of the physical constitution of matter. It seems that the solution of this problem recedes hopelessly as we advance in the path of scientific discoveries. Since atoms are not, as was formerly thought, either homogeneous or insecable—that is to say, indivisible—since they are found to consist of a nucleus around which, as around a central sun, a whole train of minutest satellites oscillate or revolve with stupendous velocity, the question now arises: What is the composition of these nuclei themselves, and what that of their electrons?

We are told by the most eminent and trustworthy physicists that the density of the nucleus of an atom of gold is so prodigious that if a woman's thimble were filled with such nuclei its weight would be something like three hundred millions of kilogrammes. We may well gasp with astonishment. Truly the world of the infinitesimally small is no less marvellous than that of the seemingly infinitely great. Man finds himself poised between these two extremes and it were difficult to decide which gives us a more sublime idea of the omnipotence of its Maker.

THE WORLD OF MATTER

Notice that all we have said thus far, and all that our great scientists tell us, leaves absolutely untouched the further question of the constitution of ether, that imponderable fluid in which we are immersed and with which are permeated all the elements of this material universe. Here is, indeed, a beautiful created image of the mysteriousness, omnipresence, invisibility, all-embracingness of God and of His sweet way of dealing with us. But, with all its stupendous recent discoveries, will not human science, faced with such enigmas, be well advised to keep an attitude of modesty and humility, and go repeating: *O God, my God, how admirable, how unsearchable Thou art in all Thy works?*

It is related in the life of St. Benedict that he once had a vision of the glory of God and that the whole universe was shown him as no bigger than a mote disporting in a sunbeam. Now, the mere fact that one is able to take in such a statement shows that the mind of man is superior to the bulk of this mighty universe, and therefore a greater world than it. It is of a different order of greatness. It is made to take in God Himself, the three Divine Persons of the Blessed Trinity; it is destined one day to see God as He is, and face to face.

Meanwhile nature and its immensity, and with the dense forest of beautiful objects it presents to our observation, is for us another garden of God, where He walks mysteriously and wishes to talk to man whom He made in His own image and likeness.

We may well fancy that it is also something like what we may call the playground of the blessed angelic natures, and one day to be also our own playground after the general resurrection, when our regenerated bodies will have put on spirituality.

Then we shall know to what end God has made such a bewildering profusion of stars. The last word about them has not yet been said. What children we are! Can we not make credit to God of a few centuries?

The whole material universe, when we look at it rightly, seems to give us an idea of the exuberant life of God and of His serenity.

It is a veil spread between the majesty of the Lord God and us, His reasonable

THE WORLD OF MATTER

creatures, a transparent veil, which if it does not allow us to discern the lineaments of His loving countenance, at least allows somewhat of the rays of His glory to pass through, so tempered that we may not be overwhelmed.

O heavenly Father: Most Holy Trinity, who hast made for Thine own glory this wondrous world of matter, I adore Thee, I thank Thee, and I love Thee!

CHAPTER XXI

The Romance of Our Little Earth

SUMMARY.—The Earth in itself an object full of interest. The abode of Godlike Man, of the Militant Church, of the Blessed Sacrament. Narrow limits within which man can exercise his sovereignty. The mystic has chosen the better part.

COMPARED with the rest of the material universe, our earth seems hardly better than a mere speck. And yet, already in itself, with the past history of its geological evolutions—every vicissitude of which is recorded in its superposed strata, if only we could read them aright—with the deeper secrets it carries in its mysterious bosom, with the wonders and riches it displays on its surface, with its inexhaustible fertility and the marvellous economy of its external structure, with its systems of mountain-ranges and rivers, its teeming manifestations of vegetative and

OUR LITTLE EARTH

animal life, with the mighty embrace and pulsations of the ocean which covers seven tenths of its surface—the earth, our little earth, is an object full of interest and well worth retaining our attention for its own sake.

It is so situated in the solar system as to make the sun, the moon, and the stars subservient to the needs of its inhabitants. Its movements of rotation on its axis and of translation around the sun give rise to the phenomena of alternate day and night and of the succession of the seasons of the year, which bring about the atmospherical conditions needful to foster and develop the whole scheme of animal and vegetative life as it revolves around man, its central figure: —man who is neither a pure spirit like the angels, nor simply a brute like the dog, the horse, a fish, a bird, or an insect, but composed of an earthly body and an immortal soul united in one person.

The real interest and dignity of the earth come precisely from its being the abode of man, of princely man, of Godlike man.

The earth is the narrow promontory from which man is expected to view the rest of

THE BURNING BUSH

the universe and read the magnificent scroll of its wonders, himself being the greatest of all, and the masterpiece of the world.

The earth is the altar of the material universe at which priestly man is expected to officiate in the name of all nature, to raise the voice of adoration and praise to the Maker of all.

The earth is the abode of the present Militant Church, the stage of the *Divina Comedia* of the dealings of God with fallen man, the place where is now carried on the *praelium magnum*, the mighty struggle between the blessed Angels and the evil spirits, of which struggle the stakes are the immortal souls of men.

The earth has seen Adam and Eve innocents, and the Son of God made Man, and His sweet Mother.

It has been drenched with His sacred Blood.

It is now the abode of His Blessed Sacrament and the scene of the perpetual Sacrifice of the Mass, as had been predicted by the prophet Malachias: *From the rising of the sun even to the going down, My Name is great among the Gentiles: and in*

OUR LITTLE EARTH

every place there is sacrifice, and there is offered to My Name a clean oblation. For My Name is great among the Gentiles, saith the Lord of Hosts (Mal. i, 11.)

The earth is the place where every man is expected to fit himself for eternal life during the short but eventful span of his temporal one; therefore whence his soul is to take its flight to heaven.

King of this material universe though he be, man at present can exercise his sovereignty but within very precise and narrow limits. This is quite providential, for, as long as we are in our present condition, we are as little children under age, who cannot be trusted, whom it is necessary to surround with all sorts of safeguards—naughty children, *enfants terribles, touche-à-tout*, who still find the means of inflicting grievous harm on themselves and others.

The surface of the earth and of the ocean, and a little below that surface (oh, very little indeed, comparatively), such is the field wherein man is free to carry out his experiments and to exercise his restless activity.

THE BURNING BUSH

The sun, the moon, and the stars are out of his reach, at a safe distance, so that he can see them and hear their message but not interfere with them, which he certainly would do if he were allowed—with what catastrophic results may be left to our imagination to picture.

Even in his narrow field of action man's control of the elemental forces of nature is but very precarious. The atmosphere, water power, steam, electricity, and all other natural agencies made use of by ourselves in mechanical contrivances, be these as ingenious as they will, ever tend to resume their natural independence, so that if the harness man has put on them happen to be weak at some point and to give way, these elementary forces are liable suddenly to kill him and toss his body away as a dead fly or a straw in a whirlwind.

Much better advised therefore, though greatly daring, the mystic when to these rash experiments he prefers that of seeking after God in the contemplation of the universe. He then finds both God and nature conspiring to forward him in his noble undertaking.

OUR LITTLE EARTH

Moreover, at the same time as things visible speak to him of the invisible ones of which they are the signs and figures, he will find that reciprocally the supernatural order of grace and glory, such as it is revealed to us by the teaching of the Church, gives him the key to the great puzzle of the material universe.

In the eyes of the mystic, nature is wholly steeped in the supernatural and illumined with a light which comes from above. Faith holds for him the torch of analogy. Has not St. Paul said: *The invisible things of Him, from the creation of the world, are clearly seen, being understood by the things that are made: His eternal power also and His Divinity* (Rom. i, 20); and again: *By faith we understand that the world was framed by the Word of God, that from invisible things visible ones might be made* (Heb. xi, 3).

The earth is the graveyard of the whole human race, its surface thick with the dust of many thousands of generations. However, the day will come when it will have to give up all its dead. And this will be but the prelude to the earth's own regeneration; for Christ is to say *Ecce nova facio omnia—Behold I make all things new* (Apoc. xxi, 5). I take it that the new earth here spoken of is the same identical planet of ours, but regenerated by fire, purified of all contamination of the sins of men, and made worthy to enter into the new heaven of God, and be a part of it for all eternity.

Were we not right in speaking of the history of our planet viewed from the time of its creation to that of its future final regeneration, as of a romance? And shall we not give due praise to God for it?

Blessed art Thou, O Lord, the God of our fathers, and worthy to be praised and glorified and exalted above all for ever, and blessed is the holy Name of Thy glory, and worthy to be praised and exalted above all in all ages.

O let the earth bless the Lord, let it praise and exalt Him above all for ever.

O all ye things that spring up in the earth, bless the Lord: praise and exalt Him above all for ever.

O all ye beasts and cattle, bless the Lord: praise and exalt Him above all for ever.

OUR LITTLE EARTH

O ye sons of men, bless the Lord: praise and exalt Him above all for ever.

O ye servants of the Lord, bless the Lord, praise and exalt Him above all for ever.

O give thanks to the Lord, because He is good, because His mercy endureth for ever and ever (Dan. iii, 52-89 *passim*).

After the general resurrection man will no longer be the inhabitant of this small planet, the earth. To that glorified son of God, the whole material universe will be given as His proper abode, to range in at liberty, by means of the wonderful qualities of spiritualized bodies: impassibility, subtilty, and agility, to which will be added that of brightness as of the sun. Through Jesus Christ, the God-made-man who is the centre of all things, and for the delight of His redeemed, the whole material universe, and, of course, the earth within it, will be assumed in glory and become part of the heavenly Jerusalem.

CHAPTER XXII

A Fallen World in Course of being Reclaimed

SUMMARY.—The human race. How God deals with it. Every man a little world. Worth and capacity of a human soul. Actual population of the globe. Rate of births and deaths. How this works out thus far, for a grand total. Our own image in God. Original sin no obstacle to the plan of God.

WE are too much accustomed to narrow views on the subject of the human race. Scarcely ever do we try to realize of what a vast multitude, actually living upon earth, we are a unit; still less do we extend our intelligent estimation of the bulk of the human race beyond the limits of the present time. And yet, those that have lived before us and died, have not gone entirely out of existence. Their souls are somewhere: even the dust of their dead bodies is not altogether vanished. It is all in the sight

A FALLEN WORLD

of God and ready to His omnipotent hand. All these men and women from the time of Adam to this day, and on to the last day of the world, all these, and we along with them, will be made to live again in the integrity of our human nature.

Thus viewed, is not the human race a great creation of God, a mighty world, a revelation of the power and the wisdom and the goodness of God, of His justice, and of His merciful ways?

God deals with the human race as a whole, and also with each one of its members individually.

God's providence governs the whole race and leads each separate member of it through the various phases of his trial to his ultimate end.

Each human individual is in himself a little world—little comparatively speaking, and yet great, very great, indeed, very unknown, almost unexplored—with wide stretches of its mysterious body, and of its still more mysterious spiritual essence, lying as so many *terrae incognitae*, which are as yet unmapped.

THE BURNING BUSH

In this region, as in others, the more we know the more do we find that there remains to be discovered. "Know thyself," urges the ancient philosopher. Ah! we are far from such knowledge. Only after the general resurrection and in the light of the Beatific Vision shall we realize the wonder that each human individual being is. He is a world, I repeat, a vast and deep world; and though his body is a comparatively small, nay, very small organized parcel of the visible universe, in his soul man transcends incomparably the whole universe of matter. A single human soul is of such worth in the eyes of Him who knows, because He made it, because He made it to His own image and likeness, that it took nothing less than the life-blood of the Son of God to redeem it. It is of such vast dimensions that the three Divine Persons want to come into it and make it their abode and take in it their delight, even now—a world still in the making, and it lies with each of us to make it, with God's help, ever so much larger and more beautiful.

And now let me try and realize that I

A FALLEN WORLD

am a mere unit of such a vast multitude of actual inhabitants of the earth; a member of a family of some two milliards of human beings actually living and breathing. Two milliards! In ciphers 2,000,000,000, and this is but an insignificant portion of the total human race, as a moment's reflection will show.

A moderate estimate of the average number of births happening daily is placed at 80,000 a day; the average death-rate being about the same.

Now see how this works out, in a year and then in a century. In multiplying those 80,000 by 360 we obtain as a result the sum of 28,800,000 (twenty-eight million eight hundred thousand) of human births in one year. Multiply this by 100, and you obtain nearly three milliards of human births; in exact number 2,880,000,000 of births in a century. If we are satisfied to stand by the chronology of Usher, the most convervative and moderate of all, and suppose that the age of the world is only 6,000 years, by multiplying these last figures by sixty we obtain the appalling sum of one hundred and

THE BURNING BUSH

seventy-two milliards and eight hundred millions of human beings. But if we take into account the fact that the uniform rate of births could not have been realized in the beginning nor directly after the Great Flood, we may, for the sake of stricter accuracy, reduce these figures by two milliards and eight hundred millions, thus obtaining, as our final grand total, the round sum of one hundred and seventy milliards of human beings created thus far.

This, of course, to say nothing of the multitude known to God alone, of those that will be born afterwards, since we do not know how long the present order of things will yet persevere. It may last a great many more centuries.

Well now, what an immense multitude is this of noble servants of God, each with an immortal soul, each made in the likeness of God, each primarily destined to know, love and serve God, each my brother, each dear to God, known of Him by name, and dealt with by Him singly, personally, and for his own sake! But what a grand idea is not this calculated to give us of the

A FALLEN WORLD

power and wisdom and sweetness of the Creator!

We have all been created innocent and holy in Adam, and an object of the love of God from all eternity, in this our primitive innocence, and every one of us destined to eternal glory.

God loved us for what He was to put in us of His own sanctity, first in the present life on earth and then later in heaven. There is in God an image of each one of us men, as God willed us to be, and this ideal image of ourselves is much better than its actual realization in existence.

Whence is this difference? It arises from the fact that on the one hand, in the making of the image of us as God loved us, God alone had a hand, and therefore made it perfect; on the other hand, in the making of our actual selves, not God alone, but, moreover, the first Adam and after him a whole line of our intermediate ancestors, and finally, our very selves, each on his own account, have had a hand.

This applies to all the children of Adam and Eve, to all the tribes of men, past, present, and future; to the white races, to the yellow ones, to the black, and to the red. Every man of us has his own image or archetype in God, and that image a noble one, and it is quite possible that our judgement will be accomplished simply by confronting what we have made ourselves into, with what God wanted to make us.

The dreadful accident to our nature, of the original sin of Adam and Eve, with its far-reaching consequences, does not stand, nevertheless, in the way of God's plan being realized. It makes it the more wonderful in its execution. All had perished in Adam, Mary, the Immaculate Virgin Mother of the Redeemer, alone excepted. Is it not worthy of the omnipotence and wisdom and sweetness of God to have changed all this *massa perdita* of the human race into a quarry from which to extract the future stones of the heavenly Jerusalem that is a-building?

All had perished in Adam, all are redeemed in Jesus Christ. Redeemed—that is to say, paid for in advance, if they will only consent to be saved. The work of hewing out one by one the elect living stones will never stop until the last of the

A FALLEN WORLD

predestinate in the Divine plan will have been consummated in sanctity.

Then will the present order of things come to an end, at the blast of the angelic trumpet by the command of the Son of Man. Then the *dead shall rise again incorruptible. Then shall come to pass the saying that is written:* DEATH IS SWALLOWED UP IN VICTORY. *O death, where is thy victory? O death, where is thy sting?* (1 Cor. xv, 52, 54, 55).

Well may we exclaim again with St. Paul:

O the depth of the riches of the wisdom and of the knowledge of God! How incomprehensible are His judgements, and how unsearchable His ways! . . . Of Him and by Him and in Him are all things; to Him be glory for ever (Rom. xi, 33, 36).

CHAPTER XXIII

THE TERRIBLE WORLD OF REPROBATION

SUMMARY.—Is God made manifest by it? Emphatically so. True the reprobates are only spoiled materials and together form a hideous chaos: but Hell itself, that is to say the place where they are imprisoned, is a real world of a stern beauty, and the work of God. The case of the reprobate. God is contrary and a torment to him. No wish to cease to be. Monuments of Divine Justice. Effusions of adoration.

THERE is a last world which we must mention among the works of God, since, indeed, it does exist; a terrible world, the Hell of the reprobates.

Is God also revealed in this work of His? Is the Blessed Trinity in some way adumbrated therein? Can we discover therein a display of the infinite perfections? Most undoubtedly.

We have already explained how each one of the blessed angelic natures, nay, each human soul of good-will, in paradise or in

THE WORLD OF REPROBATION

purgatory or on earth, is in itself a world, a real world, a world of immeasurable proportions and wellnigh infinite capacity, because made in the image of God, and possessing already within itself the three Divine Persons. However, the case is altered in the persons of fallen angels and reprobate human souls.

They do not deserve any longer to be considered as worlds in themselves. When we say "world," we mean something not only vast, but also neat and beautiful; something sweet, something organized, co-ordinated, subordinated, harmonious with itself and the rest of things created, and with its Creator; for this is the full import of the Latin term *mundus*, and of the Greek *cosmos*, which we translate by the English term "world." But these fallen ones are disordered, distorted, foul and ugly, each in his own self and all collectively. They are, in their seething multitude, cumulative disorder, carried to an unutterable paroxysm. They are an accumulation of broken worlds, of spoiled materials, absolutely unfit for anything. They are, says St. Jude, *raging waves of the sea, foaming out their confusion; wandering stars, to whom the storm of darkness is reserved for ever* (Jude i, 13). They have made themselves into this, by their own act and free choice, in open rebellion against the benevolent will and loving designs of their Creator.

But if we cannot discover in any of these wretches or their assembled multitudes the least lineament of a world, since they have made themselves into an inconceivable chaos, *a land of misery and darkness, where the shadow of death and no order, but everlasting horror dwelleth* (Job x, 22), nevertheless Hell itself—that is to say, the place which holds them within its fiery prison-walls—is assuredly the work of God, a creation of God, the handicraft of His justice, the protestation of His Sanctity and outraged love; therefore it is, indeed, yet another world, a real world, and serves as much as any of the preceding ones to reveal to us the Omnipotence, infinite Wisdom, and infinite Goodness of the Blessed Trinity.

He that can take this, let him take it (Matt. xix, 12).

THE WORLD OF REPROBATION

I know that such a view of Hell does not coincide with a certain mentality, or sentimentality, of our contemporaries. So much the worse for them. Truth must be told, even when it is terrible, nay, the more so that it is terrible. To be silent about it would be wicked, the peril of souls being so imminent and the eventual catastrophe so frightful and irreparable.

Let us try and take a clear, unbiassed view of the case of the reprobate.

First of all let us bear in mind this grand, absolutely incontrovertible principle, that everything created rests necessarily upon God, lives on God, lives to God and for Him; and that it will be so throughout all eternity. *Regem cui omnia vivunt, venite adoremus (Come let us adore the King for whom all things live);* so sings the Church perpetually.

Now, it is easy for anyone who will reflect to realize that in this necessary and eternal dependence upon God in which they are, for everything they are and have, the blessed Angels and Saints find an inexhaustible fount of joy, admiration, and gratitude. On the other hand, that same

Divine fact of their unavoidable dependence upon God will perpetually throw the reprobates into transports of the most violent rage.

The reprobates would like to be absolutely independent of God. They know that He created them—out of love and for the purposes of love—and is, therefore, their great benefactor; but they hate Him most horribly, because they find Him contrary to their perverse will.

They would like to conciliate these two contrary things: to be and at the same time to live separated from the unique wellspring of all existences. So absurd a contradiction can never be achieved in fact; hence, their insane fury. But oh! who could ever have pity on such madness? They are the authors of their own frightful misery. St. Bernard has well and tersely expressed a law of the spiritual world when he said in his treatise *De Consideratione*, Book V, that God is, both at the same time, the reward of the just and THE PUNISHMENT OF THE WICKED.

It will do us good to try to fathom this formidable mystery.

THE WORLD OF REPROBATION

By his own act the reprobate has stripped himself of all the gifts of God but one, that of existence. This last gift God alone could take away, but He never will, because it is inconsistent with His nature to annihilate anything that He has made. And the reprobate, in his own way, appreciates this one remaining gift of God.

He does not wish to return into nothingness, no, not even in order to escape the terrible punishment he has heaped upon himself, and which will be his lot for all eternity. He would never choose not to be. What he frantically wants, what he strives after with all the inflexible but also impotent strength of his will, is to be otherwise than God would have him; to be both at the same time guilty and happy, a rebel and absolutely free. Such is his craze. He stands obstinately by this perverse will of his; and so it is that God, who is all goodness and all sanctity and love, and precisely because He is all that, is contrary to the reprobate and is a torment to him.

Here below, when a miserable sinner has reached a certain degree of bodily or mental discomfort, he not infrequently lays violent and sacrilegious hands on this work of God that he himself is, in the vain attempt to force it back into non-existence. He only succeeds in making his misfortune incomparably greater and for ever final. But no sooner has he passed the threshold of the spiritual world than on this point, at least, his eyes are open: he sees so clearly what a wonderful gift existence is for a spiritual creature, that on no consideration would he now consent to be without it, were such a thing possible. It is in the realization of this fundamental, ineradicable, incorruptible benefit of existence that he finds the prodigious power of endurance called for by all the harm he has done to himself.

We may notice in this connection that Our Lord, speaking of the awful misfortune of the traitor Apostle, Judas, simply says: *It were better for him if that man had not been born* (Matt. xxvi, 24)—that is to say, if instead of coming to man's estate and incurring such a frightful guilt he had died in his mother's womb. That is precisely what even the holy man Job, in

THE WORLD OF REPROBATION

the extremity of his anguish, wished to have happened to himself, to have died before being born (Job iii, 11); but he never wished not to have been created or to return to absolute non-existence.

God has made *angels and* men INEXTERMINABLE (Wisd. iii, 11).

If they will not, by their own choice, glorify God during their trial state, by turning themselves, with the help of His grace, into monuments of His mercies, then there is no other possible alternative than this: they will have to stand for evermore as monuments of the revenge of order, of the revenge of outraged justice and sanctity.

Such will be their way of glorifying God in spite of themselves.

As I have already treated this painful subject in my third volume, *Mysticism, True and False*, chapter xviii, I beg to refer my readers to this. But I cannot leave this tremendous subject, O my God, without unburdening my soul and expressing my feelings about it.

I give thee thanks, O God, Most Holy

THE BURNING BUSH

Trinity, Father of all, our Father in heaven, I return most humble and fervent thanks to Thine infinite goodness for having resolved and decreed from all eternity to create me, to make me in Thine own image and likeness; for having loved me and thus created me and bound me to Thee by the golden and adamantine chains, marvellously supple and yet absolutely unbreakable, of my dependence upon Thee. Those chains I kiss rapturously.

I give Thee thanks also, O my God, for having so loved, from all eternity, every single one of my brethren, whether man or angel, as well the now fallen angels as the blessed ones, as well the sinners and the lost souls as Thy most faithful predestinate servants.

Thou hast created us all in love and for the purposes of love. Thou hast willed the salvation of all and each. There will, in the last end, happen to be lost only such as have obstinately refused to do Thy holy will. These wretches will never return Thee thanks; let me do it for them.

Yes, Lord, our God, Creator of heaven

and earth, of things visible and invisible, eternal thanks to Thee for the wonderful work of creation, and particularly for the gift of our spiritual nature and the boon of our endless existence!

CHAPTER XXIV

The Divine View-Point

SUMMARY.—God always right. Two adverse agencies at grips: the virus of original sin and the grace of redemption. Various oppositions. The alternative before us. In the hands of our free will. How sin itself turns to the glory of God.

HERE is a beautiful saying of Mgr. d'Hulst, the first Rector of the present Catholic University of Paris: "*La sagesse consiste à donner raison à Dieu en toute chose,*" which means: Wisdom consists in always finding that God is right. God is always right. It must be so, otherwise God would not be God. Therefore wisdom indeed, for a reasonable creature, consists ever and from the very first—*à priori*, as the philosophers express it—in taking the part of God, in placing oneself at the view-point of God, for a due appreciation of all things.

It is easy to perceive how such a way of

THE DIVINE VIEW-POINT

acting is calculated to raise a man above himself and all things created, to flood his mind with light and to pacify him.

For such a man, whatever may betide, all is well and nothing can disturb him. St. Teresa has celebrated this fact in a charming poem of a few lines, beginning, if I remember rightly, with the words: "Nada te disturbe, nada te espanta." The Holy Ghost has put it tersely thus: *Say to the just man that it is well* (Isa. iii, 10).

It is well; it is well, even though I may not understand it. I trust it all to God, I know that He knows it all, that He cannot be outwitted by the evil one. My soul, all's well!

When by grace of the Holy Spirit a man finds himself in such a frame of mind, he can face any situation, look serenely upon any contingency whatever, he can meet unperturbed any tragical event, being fully convinced that God, the good and loving God, will have the last word, and that in the end all will turn to His glory and to the good of His predestinate.

As far as we men here below are concerned, it is easy to see from the view-point

THE BURNING BUSH

of God that all the various events of history have reference exclusively to two mighty agencies ever active and ever at grips one with the other—these, namely, on the one hand the virus of original sin; on the other, the grace of Divine redemption.

All the personal sins of men, all the antagonisms of civilized nations, all the degradations of savage peoples, all is explained by the poison of original sin, inoculated into every individual person, manifesting its malignity in various ways according to the diversities of time and circumstance.

Now, God in His wisdom has decreed that the remedy to this virus should come out of the very bowels of humanity, through Our Lord Jesus Christ and His Immaculate Virgin Mother, Mary. And further, it has pleased God to decree that this remedy or counter-poison should be administered by a set of men officially deputed to this work—namely, the priests, and carried to all the ends of the earth by the missionaries of the Catholic Church.

Says the wise son of Sirach in the Book of Ecclesiasticus: *Good is set against evil*

THE DIVINE VIEW-POINT

and life against death; so also is the sinner against a just man. And so look upon all the works of the Most High, two and two and one against another (Eccli. xxxiii, 15).

Against Lucifer and his crew of fallen rebel spirits there stood Michael and the dazzling phalanx of all the blessed Angels.

Adam and Eve, the guilty ancestors of the whole human race, are offset by the new Adam, Jesus, and the new Eve, Mary.

Over against the fatal tree of the knowledge of good and evil which caused our death, there is planted in the midst of the Church the Cross of Our Lord, the fruit of which brings the souls of men to live again, nay, to a higher and more opulent kind of life.

Against the Babylon of this world of sin with the synagogue of the children of the devil, there stands the Militant Church of Christ, made up of all the men of goodwill, who are, indeed, the true sons of God.

To the nefarious maxims of the world is opposed the Gospel of Our Lord Jesus Christ, with His new commandment of brotherly love, His Counsels of Perfection, and His eight Beatitudes.

To the three concupiscences, that of the eyes, that of the flesh, and the pride of life, are opposed Faith, Hope, Charity, together with the four infused moral virtues and the seven gifts of the Holy Ghost.

Whosoever will not freely receive the mercy of God will perforce experience His justice. Whosoever will not allow God to save him will be damned. Of two things, one, we must embrace either love or hatred; either the glory of Heaven or the flames of Hell; either personal holiness in the company of all the blessed, or the foul ugliness and incurable perversity of sin in the company of all the reprobates. Such is the alternative.

Thus has the good and loving God placed the angel first and then man, in the hands of their own free will.

Before each one, during the time of his trial, has been set good and evil, and it is for each freely to choose. God wants us to make a good choice; to this end he presses His grace upon all: those who chose aright, owe it to the help of the grace of God; those who chose amiss have only themselves to blame.

THE DIVINE VIEW-POINT

But whatever be the choice of the ones and the others, it all turns in the end to the glory of God.

Sin itself turns to the glory of God.

Sin itself, whether in time or in eternity, turns to the glory of God.

It is a great glory to God when, after a long life of evil deeds, a poor sinner does at last repent.

It is a great glory to God that all the sins of the world have been atoned for by the death of Our Lord on the Cross and that reparation has been offered to the majesty of God, infinitely greater than the offence.

It is great glory to God that all those who will not repent will be finally wiped out of the face of the fair world and dumped into the pit of Hell, where they will be for ever punished, although not as much as they deserve.

Let, therefore, no one be scandalized and ask, as casting a doubt upon the goodness of the Supreme Judge: Oh, why has God allowed the great evil of sin to take place?

My son, the good and loving God has permitted the great evil of sin in view of the greater good of the expiation of sin, of the repentance of the sinner, of the display of God's mercies, and for those who will not have mercy, of the display of His justice.

The mystic, the contemplative, the lover of God sees things and judges of them as God sees them and judges of them. He cannot but be right, absolutely right.

O my God, Most Holy Trinity, Father, Son, and Holy Ghost; Creator, Redeemer, and Sanctifier, Thine oracle in the Book of Wisdom (i, 1) hath given us this warning: *Think of the Lord in goodness.* This I want to do ever and for ever. Indeed, I confess it with fear and trembling and also with boundless joy: *Thou art just, O Lord, and Thy judgement is right* (Ps. cxviii, 137). Be Thou blessed *in aeternum et ultra* (Exod. xv, 18).

CHAPTER XXV

THE DIVINE SOLITARINESS IN THE MIDST OF CREATION

SUMMARY.—Immanence and Transcendence—two aspects of a Divine fact. What these words mean. God ever creating—intimately present in every parcel of the universe. The six days of Genesis and the natural laws. St. Augustine on miracles. God our centre where we can meet. The full import of the term transcendence. Theologians and mystical writers on this subject. Fundamental nothingness of all that is not God. That God is His own all sufficing company in the Trinity of His Persons.

THIS chapter will, unless we greatly mistake, prove to be, at least, as interesting as any of the foregoing ones, in spite of its being more metaphysical. In order to make it quite easy to understand, I have carefully sifted and separated its various elements and divided it into separate sections, which ought to be read in their order, being careful not to pass to the next until the preceding one has been mastered.

THE BURNING BUSH

I.

The contemplation of God in His works, in the refulgent mirror of creation, not only bears witness to His infinite perfections, especially to His omnipotence and wisdom and sweetness, which shine forth everywhere and in everything, and to His ineffable justice and mercy in His dealings with angels and men, but it serves, moreover, to manifest and to bring home to our minds the two very striking properties of the Divine Essence which theologians call Immanence and Transcendence.

Let us not be frightened by these two philosophical terms. They have a very beautiful import and are easily understood. They simply mean that God is, on the one hand, necessarily present in all things; and on the other hand, infinitely above all things.

If God had not created anything, or if we had confined ourselves to the contemplation of God in Himself, this twofold sublime property of His would have remained hidden in Him for ever unknown and unknowable. This shows that by our contemplation of God in His works we

THE DIVINE SOLITARINESS

have gained a distinct addition to our knowledge of Him.

The Immanence and Transcendence of God are two aspects of a Divine fact that will stand for evermore and will be an inexhaustible source of admiration to the blessed in heaven. But there is no reason why we ourselves, while still on earth, should not begin even now to make it also the subject of our loving contemplation.

Immanence, then, is that exclusive property of the Divine Essence by which God is intimately present, of His presence of power, in everything created; Transcendence is that Divine property by which God is absolutely independent of all the natural laws of time and space and is above all modes of being and acting of His creatures, so that He absolutely surpasses them, and, so to speak, extends beyond them infinitely.

II.

God is in the midst of creation, in the whole of it, and in every part of it, not, indeed, as its soul, as though He were a component part of the universe, as the

THE BURNING BUSH

Pantheists would have us believe, but as its first cause, *Prima Causa.*

God is ever creating the world and every separate item of it. *My Father worketh until now, and I work,* replied Jesus to the Jews who were finding fault with Him for having healed on the Sabbath Day a man *who had been thirty years under his infirmity* (John v, 5-17).

It were an error to think that in order to discover God in the act of creating we need go back through all intervening centuries to the work of the six days of Genesis, to the very beginning of all things. Even now, at this moment, at every moment, nothing whatever would persevere in existence were not Almighty God perpetually creating it. Every object in nature, the earth, the sea, the sky, the stars; every person in the world, man or angel, every separate soul, at every moment, in every respect, has need of God in order to continue in being. You, my dear friend, would not be at present reading this, for you would not exist at all, were not God actually creating you at this very moment.

THE DIVINE SOLITARINESS

Wheresoever is found some being, spiritual or corporeal, great or small, there God also is with His omnipotence, infinite majesty, ineffable sweetness, in the august Trinity of His Persons. If He were not there, that thing could never be. In order to exist, even the tiniest thing imaginable calls for the previous and simultaneous existence of God, His intimate presence within it, and His perpetual creative action upon it. In order to be at all, that thing has need of God, and, therefore, however insignificant it may be, it is, nevertheless, an irrefutable demonstration of God.

I am, therefore God is.

And, O my God, I confess that I am in duty bound to worship Thee present in me, sustaining me in existence, enveloping me on all sides, so that I do not know which to admire most, either that Thou, O my God, art in me, or that I am in Thee. *He is not far from everyone of us, for in Him we live, and move, and be* (Acts xvii, 28).

III.

It might perhaps be asked: What then has Almighty God done in the beginning and in the six days of Genesis more than He is now doing?

The reply is that He then drew out of pure nothingness the materials of this visible universe at the same time as all the angelic natures, and established the order of secondary causes and the harmonious workings of the natural laws.

But, all this notwithstanding, it remains that, under the warp and woof of the secondary causes and natural laws which have held good through so many centuries and centuries of centuries, God stands revealed as the First Cause, whose active influx is perpetually at work and absolutely necessary. *Rerum Deus tenax vigor*, sings Holy Church in the liturgy. God is the Almighty Agent who gives to all things their virtue, at the same time as He is the centre which keeps things in themselves and binds them all in one universe.

Here is the proper place to recall a familiar saying of St. Augustine, to the effect that the natural laws of the world—though we pay so little attention to them through being used to their smooth workings—are much more stupendous than any

THE DIVINE SOLITARINESS

miracle or all the miracles put together. Miracles, be they ever so wonderful, are after all but casual interventions of God, limited in time and space, whilst the laws of nature and the continuance of the universe in existence call for an active exercise of God's omnipotence, co-extensive in time and space with the whole history of the world past, present, and future.

The forty years' duration of the miracle of the manna was, indeed, a great wonder; so was also the miraculous multiplication of the five loaves with which Our Lord fed the more than five thousand people in the desert: but a far greater wonder is the way in which God feeds all His creatures through the harmonious workings of natural laws. Every day since the beginning of the world, all living things cry out to God, each in its own language: *Our Father who art in heaven, give us this day our daily bread:* and through this long succession of centuries God has never failed to supply the varied wants of this immense family of beasts and men spread over the whole earth.

IV.

The foregoing considerations duly weighed will strike one with awe and reverence. But there is a peculiar aspect of this great truth that God is the centre of all His creatures, which may perhaps more powerfully stir in us feelings of gratitude and tender love towards Him.

Is it not a very touching, affecting thought, to consider that to all His children scattered in the broad expanse of the Church Militant, Suffering and Triumphant, our good and loving Heavenly Father is a trysting-place where we can, with the most absolute certainty, meet and come into contact with one another—under the veil of faith, of course, as far as we on earth are concerned?

Then, from this fact that our good and loving God is Himself the binding force and the link of union of all persons and things, does it not seem that our dear dead are now a great deal nearer to us than when they were in life?

When they were still on earth, a wall was enough to keep them separated from us

THE DIVINE SOLITARINESS

and to prevent our actual intercourse with them. Still more so if they happened to be at a great distance. But now, if I so will, I can have speech with my dear departed ones, whenever and as long as I will. Whether they be in Purgatory, or already in the glory of Paradise, makes but little difference, I can meet them in God, and although it is not given me to hear them, I am quite sure to be heard of them, God Himself being our unfailing intermediary.

V.

Now we come at last to the real gist of this chapter, to the summit towards which we have been slowly climbing.

In order to bring home to our reader the full import of the term *transcendence* as applied to God, we cannot do better than reproduce a very apt saying of St. Thomas Aquinas. It occurs in the First Part of his *Summa Theologica* (Quaestio XXXI, art. iii, *ad* 1). There the Angelic Doctor explains that if there was not in the Divine Essence a plurality of Persons, we should have to say that God, even in the midst of His blessed Angels and Saints, is alone and solitary. "For," says he, "the solitude of a person is not broken by the fact of his associating with things of a different nature. Thus, we say of a man that he is alone in the garden, although he be there surrounded with numberless animals and plants. In the same way, if there were no plurality of Divine Persons, we should have to pronounce that God is alone or solitary, even though there exist now with Him angels and men in numberless multitudes."

Hence, when we say with Holy Church, after St. Paul (1 Tim. i, 7), *Soli Deo honor et gloria*, it does not mean only: To God alone be praise and glory, to the exclusion of anyone else, but, moreover: To God who is alone, to God who has no like. "Who is like unto God," exclaimed the Archangel Michael, when Lucifer would have raised his throne by the side of the Most High (Isa. xiv, 13; Apoc. xii, 7). God is without His like in the majesty of His Divine Essence and Substance and Life. HE TRANSCENDS ALL.

It is also in this sense that we must understand this passage of the Book of

THE DIVINE SOLITARINESS

Job (xiv, 4): *Who can make him clean, that is conceived of unclean seed? Nonne tu qui solus es?* Our Douay version translates these last words thus: "Is it not Thou who only art?" But I think one is justified in finding that this does not render the full meaning either of the Latin, or of the Septuagint, or of the Hebrew original, for they all imply and convey that forcible thought of the absolute transcendence of God as shown by *His magnificent solitariness.*

VI.

In order to do justice, as far as possible, to this wonderful attribute of God, His absolute Transcendence and consequent Solitariness, theologians warn us that all we say of the Divine Essence is said only equivocally, not univocally. This means that, for want of a better mode of expressing ourselves, we are compelled to make use of a word which does not really fit the subject, and which, therefore, must not be taken too literally.

This is the reason also why mystical writers like the Pseudo-Areopagite coin very extraordinary expressions when discoursing about God, speaking of His *superessence, supersubstance, supersubsistence*, and so on. All this means that God is a substance in a sense infinitely superior to that of the substances we know; that He has an essence without a parallel; that the words "Persons, hypostases" have here infinitely larger meanings than when applied to man or angel; that the numerals in God denote something transcending our human counting, for, indeed, God is so One that He has no second, and He is Three in One in a way of which no created things could ever present an example.

My God, O Father, Son, and Holy Ghost, O Thou unspeakable, O Thou "Anonumos, Panonumos, Hyperonumos," as Thy illustrious servant, St. Gregory Nazianzen, tells us Thou art; yes, "The One without a name, in whom all things are named, who transcendeth all names," my God, my God, my God, oh, how I must worship Thee!

THE DIVINE SOLITARINESS
VII.

Now, now, indeed, do I begin to understand this great truth that Thou art All, whilst compared with Thee, all things created are simply nothing. Yes, nothing, nothing, nothing!

What dost thou say, O my soul? Has it not seemed to us at times that we were a very big thing, a very important parcel of the universe, a wonderful personage? What a ludicrous error! Before God the whole universe is not even as a drop of water compared to the ocean, not even as a grain of sand. If so of the whole universe, what shall we say of tiny me? I am nothing, I am he that is not: such is the truth; *for*, says St. Paul, *if any man think himself to be something, whereas he is nothing, he deceiveth himself* (Gal. vi, 3).

Greatness of God, nothingness of all that is not God, nothingness of myself. An aboriginal nothingness, a fundamental nothingness, a perpetual tendency to return into nothingness, a perpetual need that God should uphold me and prevent me from falling back into nothingness; such is my case.

VIII.

Now to conclude.

If in the midst of His wonderful works, in the midst of this universe of things visible and invisible, of myriads and myriads of angels and men, God is All Alone, All by Himself, and the Only One that is—even as He proclaims it out of the burning bush in these solemn words *I am who am*—if, I say, there is around His infinite Majesty an awful, unbroken, unviolable solitude, yet let us bear in mind that God is not in loneliness. He is to Himself His own company. The fulness of His own Divine life is such that He subsists in three distinct Persons, most loving and all sufficing to one another's infinite delight.

O God, O Father, Son, and Holy Ghost, *de profundis, out of the depths* of my native nothingness, I cry out to Thee; I adore Thine infinite Being, I love Thy marvellous Life and All-sufficiency to Thyself. I humbly desire to build myself upon Thee. Outside of Thee nothing can stand. *Dominus firmamentum meum* (Ps. xvii, 3). O my great wonderful God!

PART III—GOD IN THE HEART OF THE MYSTIC

CHAPTER XXVI

Introductory to this Third Part

SUMMARY.—That one does not know God until one has viewed Him under this aspect. This treatise would not be complete without such a presentment of God. Inspired writers and saintly authors have opened the way. A prejudice that has to be broken down.

IN this Third Part I have endeavoured to draw for the edification of my reader some picture, however faint and feeble, of the wonderful familiarity with which the Lord God, so good and loving, is wont to deal with a soul of good-will.

One does not know God until one has viewed Him under this particular aspect.

Among the divinely inspired writers, at least two have shown us, in a lively manner, the loving intercourse which takes place between God and the fervent soul: the first is King David in the Book of Psalms, the second is the writer of the Canticle of Canticles. And then, from among the works of the Saints, let it suffice to name, as specimens of this sort of literature, the celebrated *Confessions* of St. Augustine, the Third Book of the *Imitation of Christ*, and the *Living Flame of Love* of St. John of the Cross.

What these authors have so excellently done I have felt constrained, in spite of my own unworthiness and incapacity, to attempt on my own account and in my own way, because a work on the Ecstatic Contemplation of the Blessed Trinity would not be complete without such a description.

I set down some phases of the little drama of Divine love as I have been privileged more than once to see it enacted. I set it down with simplicity, as I understand it, as I have had some personal experience of it. Let people make of it what they please.

There will, no doubt, be those who will think that I have been drawing on my imagination to an unwarranted extent. I can but reply that, on the contrary, I am only too conscious of remaining almost at an infinite distance from the Divine realities of which I would like to give them a taste.

INTRODUCTION TO THIRD PART

Others may be inclined to take scandal at seeing *the secrets of the King* set down in black and white, in homely phrase, in the vulgar language of our every-day intercourse with each other. They may think this a desecration, even though it be done for their own use and edification. But there can be no greater error than this.

What! *The children of the devil*, as Our Lord calls those who will not follow Him (John viii, 44), may describe and sing in prose and poetry, as complacently as they like, their impure love-stories and give to all who read them the thrill of guilty pleasure: and one should not be allowed to make known and to celebrate the sweet, inebriating joys of Divine love; to try and picture them as best one can and make others share them!

O cursed world which has succeeded in deceiving even *the children of light* to such an extent, and imposing on them as an axiom that the beautiful things of God and the good things of God ought to be kept carefully concealed, even as something to be ashamed of! Is it not high time for us to break the despotic yoke of such a prejudice? Is it not high time that we should dare to use our liberty of true children of God, and to make an open profession, not only of our faith and of the hope that is in us, but also of our love, of our love I say, of our love of God who made us and who is so good and loving and sweet?

As on a former occasion (cf. *Divine Contemplation for All*, chapters xxii-xxv), I have been obliged in this Third Part, here and there, to employ figurative language as the best means of conveying my meaning. No one, I am sure, will find fault with me for this, for it is impossible to mistake the true import of it all.

CHAPTER XXVII

The Marvellous Adventure

SUMMARY.—That few seek after God. How thrilling this adventure compared to all others. Its wide range. It captivates the whole man. What it reveals to him.

FEW there are, nowadays, who seek after God. People seek after self and after all sorts of consolations from created things. The few, the very few, who care not for such consolations and who do really seek after God are the mystics, the genuine contemplatives. Oh, these are the happy ones!

The earnest search after God, by a pilgrim of the earth, and what follows upon the finding, constitute positively the most marvellous adventure that can ever be thought of.

A thrilling adventure, full of poignant interest, fruitful in unforeseen developments and striking situations, bringing about most sweet and comforting im-

THE BURNING BUSH

mediate results, to say nothing of its entrancing ultimate consequences which reach out far beyond present and future times, even unto farthest eternity.

In comparison with this, what are the other adventures, mythical or real, of which mention is made in the literatures of the world?

The search of the Golden Fleece by the Argonauts, that of the Holy Grail by the Knights of the Round Table; the conquest of the Holy Sepulchre by the Crusaders of the Middle Ages; the discovery of the New World by Christopher Columbus, that of the Pacific Ocean by Balboa, the conquest of Peru by Pizarro; the search after the so-called Philosopher's Stone, or after the Spring of Perpetual Youth, or after the lost Atlantides; the voyages to the North Pole, or to the South Pole by our daring explorers, the perilous journey to Lhassa, or to Mecca, or to Timbuctu by Europeans, the ascent of Mount Everest, the discovery of the Tomb of Pharaoh Tutankhamen with its buried treasures; or, on a lower plane, the fast and furious race after fortune, fame, honours, the pleasures

THE MARVELLOUS ADVENTURE

of the flesh, or the more refined ones of the mind: what are all those adventures, either in themselves or in their results, that could bear comparison with the marvellous adventure of the search after God?

The search after God ranges all over the earth, all over the stars and goes beyond, and yet is achieved at home, in the secret of the heart, and by men whom one would hardly describe as daring spirits, though, indeed, they are the most daring spirits in existence.

The search after God captivates at the same time the mind, the heart, the senses—the whole man, body and soul—of the searcher. It attunes him to the music of the heavenly spheres and choirs angelical.

It reveals in him depths hitherto unsuspected and capabilities wellnigh infinite; nay, and gives them fulfilment. For it brings that happy seeker suddenly face to face and hand to hand, with Him who is the goal of his fond audacious quest.

CHAPTER XXVIII

What Happens Then

SUMMARY.—When an earthly lover meets his beloved. With the Mystic in search of God the process is reversed. Beginning of the little love drama.

WE all know what does happen when an earthly lover at last meets with the idol of his dreams. Does he not, at once, come to a dead stop? See him stand still, silent, motionless, though bubbling over with hardly suppressed feelings, eagerly gorging himself with the sight. Oh! he is, at least for the time being, a contemplative.

The next stage is for him to impress the image of his beloved deep into his heart, and carry it with him wheresoever he goes, and, losing sight of everything but this object of his adoration, to prostrate before it his whole being.

But the silence cannot last. Soon, very

WHAT HAPPENS THEN

soon, the wounded mortal who has received deeply into his heart the flaming arrow of love cannot bear his joy in silence: he is constrained to give vent to his tumultuous feelings. He must talk, he must sing of her whose charms enthral him.

At this point even the less skilled man will rise to the lyrical mood and show himself both poet and musician. With his heart for a musical instrument, on which are stretched the delicate, strong, vibrating chords of his sensitiveness, he begins to play as never did artist upon flute, harp, or violin, and his whole soul passes in the melody.

Now, this is but a faint adumbration of what happens to the fervent Christian who has really fallen in love with God. Only in his case the process is reversed: the beauties of God dawn upon him but little by little, and for this reason praise goes first, slowly rising to its climax, and then, at last, at last, there comes silent enjoyment, deep, and inexpressible.

Yes, no sooner has the lover of God been given a taste of the sweetness of the Divine Majesty, than he cannot sing its praise loud enough for his own satisfaction. To relieve his pent-up feelings he must needs proclaim to all the world his passionate love and admiration and overflowing joy. Soon, however, a new mood intervenes: a spell is cast upon him. One by one the chords of his lyre are pressed by the finger of the Spirit and silenced. The hermit-soul withdraws to its cave in the innermost depth of its own self; there to enjoy God in utmost privacy and far from any profane gaze.

Then it is, then and there, and with these circumstances of silence and secrecy, that begins in earnest the little love drama.

CHAPTER XXIX

THE ENCOUNTER

SUMMARY.—What takes place in the secret of the Soul. Transports of joy and illusions. Darkness and Desolation. What to do then. Gold in the crucible.

NOW the fervid lover seizes upon God as upon a prey and gives himself up wholly, unreservedly, to the devouring, all-consuming exigencies of this *Beloved of the beloved*. But oh, with what transports of joy!

Made bold by the darkness, he dares to embrace his All-Beloved, to kiss Him, shedding burning tears and stammering to Him his love in broken accents. He feels also the loving embrace of God, though unable to see Him. He feels His touch and is thrilled to the innermost of his soul. He hears the soft whisper of His voice and catches upon his own lips the breath, the sweet-scented breath of His mouth. *Let Him kiss me with the kiss of His mouth,* exclaims the bride in the Canticle of Canticles. Ah! no wonder, then, no wonder that our Lover should faint, quite overpowered by heavenly delight. Is he still on earth or already in heaven? He could not tell. All he knows is that he has surely found the object of his venturesome, daring quest. All hardships are forgotten. In the wild, extravagant joy of his heart he cries out: *Tenui eum nec dimittam:* I have got hold of my God and my Love; I shall not let him go. No; never!

Puny one, what art thou saying? Does it lie with thee to hold Him fast? Thinkest thou hast already left this land of exile and reached *the land of Promise?* Come down again to the hard and harsh realities of the present life. Behold, all of a sudden thy beloved Lord, the Most Holy God of heaven, disentangles Himself from thy embrace and takes Himself away. Thou art still with Him; He has not ceased to be with thee, but He hides Himself. He seems to have receded far, far away; and thou, in consequence, art left utterly desolate. Oh! this is a cruel turn of affairs. Now what shalt thou do?

THE ENCOUNTER

Indeed, what is to be done?

Simply this. Thou must begin all over again the search after God: set out again in quest of thy Beloved and spare no pains and give thyself no repose until He be found again. Call for Him unabashed and tireless, and steadily refuse the consolations of creatures. We have had already our experiences of the mysterious withdrawal of the Beloved in our contemplation of the Sacred Humanity of Our Lord (cf. *Mystical Initiation*, chapters xxviii and xxxii). Now we are dealing with God in His pure Divine Essence: we are made to witness His Divine playfulness with the soul of a lowly pilgrim of the earth. It is almost a repetition of the same incidents, but still more intensely felt, more soul-stirring, precisely because more purely spiritual, nay, altogether Divine. Such a new quest after our All-beloved, begun in sorrow, will yield the more joy when we find Him again.

And so it goes on during the earthly life of the child of Divine love.

In thus passing alternately from intensest joy to deepest sorrow, and back again, in

THE BURNING BUSH

God's good time, into heavenly rapture, followed again by a cruel sense of dereliction sometimes verging on despair, the pilgrim soul is being refined as gold in the crucible. She grows pure, bright, dazzling bright and strong, more and more beautiful in the eyes of God and His blessed Angels, and heaps up a mountain of eternal merits at the same time as she advances in experimental, mystical, intimate knowledge of God.

Never more, after this drastic, energetic treatment by fire, will she yield to the temptation of discouragement, or will she slacken her pace on the rugged path of sanctity, until the shadows of this land of exile retire before the splendours of the Beatific Vision: *donec aspiret dies et inclinentur umbrae* (Cant. ii, 17).

CHAPTER XXX

A Challenge

SUMMARY.—The Key of the lives of the Saints. The Soul's reply. The Roman Coliseum. Another Coliseum not made by human hands. The spectators. The spectacle. The Lord is a Warrior. What dost thou say?

IN the search after God, such as we have been endeavouring to sketch it out in the foregoing chapters, is found the key to the lives of the dear Saints and of many a great lover of God who has passed away from this world unnoticed and unrecorded. Thus it has been with them in past ages; thus it is at this very moment for generous souls, known of God alone, scattered all over the world. Thus will it be for ourselves last and least of all, provided only that we be willing.

Nothing more is required of us at the start. We have only to set out on the marvellous quest with a burning desire. The good and loving God who by His prevenient grace gives us already so to will and to set about it is sure to assist us all along and to crown our feeble efforts with a glorious measure of success.

Now what sayest thou to this, O Christian soul?

With utmost alacrity the soul replies: *Dixi, nunc coepi* (Ps. lxxvi, 11). I am resolved. I want to attempt the wonderful adventure. Let me set about the quest after God without a moment's delay. I do desire to keep steadily at it, until I have found Him *whom my soul loveth.*

Well said, O my Christian. And now, in order still further to strengthen thee in thy noble resolve, hear something about the scene of thy future valiant deeds and about those who shall witness them. For, indeed, it is a grand sight, a sort of pompous show and exhibition which, all unknown to himself, the fervent Christian is offering to the blessed Angels and the Saints of Paradise —*spectaculum . . . angelis* (1 Cor. iv, 9) —when he enters upon the wonderful quest after God. A magnificent spectacle, wholly spiritual, wholly supernatural, wholly Divine.

When, some twenty-five years ago, I was

A CHALLENGE

in Rome, I loved to visit the immense ruin of the Coliseum, and each time it was with fresh feelings of wonder. My particular delight was to climb up to the highest tier, where that was still possible, and to reconstitute in imagination the stupendous structure, as it must have looked in the days of its pristine splendour and integrity.

What a genius of a man must have been the Jewish captive who planned this well-named colossus of a building, and who at the same time contrived to give it, both inside and out, the light, airy, elegant form of a flower basket!

Gathered and seated at ease within its prodigious depths, the whole free population of ancient Rome—from the emperor, surrounded with his gilded court, down to the meanest rank of the plebeian in his rags—was wont to forget, at least for the time being, all other business but that of greedily devouring with their eyes the spectacles offered in the arena below: bloody fights of gladiators, or abominable buffooneries, or the much appreciated, toothsome amusement of seeing Christians thrown to the lions and by them devoured

THE BURNING BUSH

alive, as was the case with the aged Bishop of Antioch, the great Ignatius.

When particularly pleasing incidents took place, the applause and vociferations of the immense multitude would break forth and roll out as peals of thunder, to give vent to the feelings of the insane and ferocious enjoyment of these people.

Let us now picture to ourselves another Coliseum, in shape infinitely more noble and elegant and of incomparably vaster proportions—*cujus artifex et conditor Deus* (Heb. xi, 10)—whereof Divine love is the architect and the builder. On its lofty steps, tier after tier, range themselves the all but infinite multitude of the blessed Angels and of the Saints, with King Jesus, Our Lord, in their midst, throned under a gorgeous canopy, and having at His right hand our Lady, His sweet Virgin-Mother, Queen of heaven.

All are intently gazing downwards.

What is there in the vast arena so to rivet their attention? Only this: a solitary man, a fervent Christian, who with burning desire is setting forth upon the great adventure of the search after God; a puny

A CHALLENGE

human being in the infirm condition of the present life, bold enough to challenge the Lord of heaven to come to grips with himself.

He goes forth blindfolded, with hands outstretched, seeking his quarry, if we may use the expression. And the Tri-une God, the Lord of heaven, does not disdain to step down into the arena, clad as a warrior, having on the breast-plate of His infinite goodness, and to wrestle with this child of clay. *The Lord is a warrior: Dominus vir pugnator* (Exod. xv, 3)—a warrior who not only fights against His enemies, but who, moreover, likes to wrestle with His dearest friends, to play with them the exciting game of love.

Now, God meets halfway the man who seeks Him. He allows Himself to be seized upon, and, in a way, held down, at least, for a short space. Anon He will extricate Himself from the close embrace of His loving adversary and evade for a while his ardent blind pursuit. Then again, at a turn, He will let Himself be overtaken and seized and held captive in the frail bands of a creature's fond embrace.

Who will tell us how such a spectacle stirs to their utmost depths the feelings of admiration and sympathy of the heavenly citizens? They cannot take away their eyes from it. With unstinted applause and loud acclamations, they underline the varying incidents of the little drama as it unwinds itself and progresses to its climax. But our hero, in his present condition of a pilgrim of the earth, neither sees nor hears them.

Well, now, it lies with each of us to offer such a spectacle to the blessed Angels and Saints. I ask yet again: What dost thou say, O soul of good-will? *Amici auscultant* (Cant. viii, 13). All heaven is listening, eager to catch every word from thy lips. They have already anticipated what thy ready answer will be. Now what they want is to see thee boldly step into the arena. Are not acts the best proof of our noble intent?

CHAPTER XXXI

Gladness in the Morning

SUMMARY.—Weeping in the evening, and its remedy. A vision in a dream. The three Divine Persons and a little boy. A question. The reply. Waking up and after.

AT the end of a long protracted, unbroken period of cruel darkness and desolation, as I was seeking some relief in gathering various texts of Holy Writ to lay as a cordial upon my aching heart, my attention was particularly drawn to that of St. Peter wherein he affirms that we are *made partakers of the Divine nature* (2 Pet. i, 4); and also to this wonderful promise of Our Lord in the Apocalypse: *To him that shall overcome, I will give to sit with Me in My throne: as I also have overcome and am set down with My Father in His throne* (Apoc. iii, 21); and to His warning us in the Gospel that unless we become as little children we shall not enter into the kingdom of heaven (Matt. xviii, 3);

and finally, to this oracle of Psalm xxix, verse 6: *In the evening weeping shall have place, and in the morning gladness.* At last tired out I fell asleep and had a dream.

I saw a great throne of gold and ivory on which were seated together three Persons, God the Father, God the Son, and between them a lovely little boy of six or seven years:

God the Father, in gorgeous overflowing robes, crowned with a tiara, His face breathing calm majesty.

God the Son, Our Lord, with a glorious kingly crown on His head, clad in loose white garments, which left a good deal of His glorified Sacred Humanity bare; His face radiant with inexpressible benevolence.

The boy, dressed as a little prince, with a graceful countenance, his head crowned with a golden circlet, his curly hair falling on his shoulders. He was straining to his breast, with both hands, a white dove, with wings outstretched, the Divine Dove, the Holy Ghost.

And it was given me to perceive that from the heart of God the Father, and from the heart of God the Son, and from the

GLADNESS IN THE MORNING

heart of God the Holy Ghost, tendrils, as it were, of vine were shooting forth and intertwining around the heart of the little fellow, and he looked the picture of happiness, but of such happiness as is not of this world.

His lips were moving. I intently listened to catch the sound of his words. Then I heard him softly repeating to himself:

"*O Father, Son, and Holy Ghost!*"

Three times he repeated this ejaculation, as one beside himself, and tears of joy, round as pearls, swiftly ran down his cheeks and on his garment.

I could not help it: I had to cry out:

"Happy that child! But who is he?"

Then a voice behind me (was it that of my guardian angel?) answered:

"It is even thee, if thou wilt."

Whereupon I woke up and found that all my trouble of the previous night had vanished as smoke, or been rolled away as clouds, and it was full daylight and gladness in my soul.

Ever, ever since that blissful dream, I see my God and little me together, and my heart warbles within me as a bird—warbles a wild song of adoration and love, a song of a few notes; no other words than these:

"O Father, Son, and Holy Ghost!"

But oh, with what depth of meaning, and of feeling! with what rapturous melody!

CHAPTER XXXII

THE GOLDEN PYRAMID

SUMMARY.—Gird up thy loins. What for. The Knight in the Palace of Quiet. What he wishes to see. The Holy Trinity under the symbolical appearance of a Pyramid. Petition of Fidelis.

LO, I seem to hear within me again that imperious, most sweet, compelling voice, which I heard at least once before.

"*Gird up thy loins like a man,*" it says (Job xxxviii, 3).

And again:

"*Thou hast yet a great way to go*" (3 Kings xix, 7).

With a gladness born of the grace of God, the instant reply rises to my lips:

"*Here I am, O Lord, ready to do Thy bidding*" (Ps. cxviii, 66)—*Where is Thy servant to go?*" (Isa. vi, 8).

And the voice:

"Thou art not to go anywhere with thy bodily feet, but to speak to thy brethren, so as to be heard to the farthest ends of the earth. 'Let thy tongue be *the pen of a scrivener that writeth swiftly*'" (Ps. xliv, 2). Some pages there be which are the very life of the human race, lifting men up to a higher plane. Do thou write such another page.

And I again, with utmost alacrity, not unmixed with a sense of awe and self-abasement:

"O Lord, *da quod jubes et jube quod vis:* Do Thou grant me Thy grace, that I may be able to fulfil Thy command."

It is all about the Knight in the Palace of Quiet, of whom much has been said already in our fourth volume (cf. *Divine Contemplation for All*, chapters xxi to xxv inclusive).

He has now for a long time, year after year, enjoyed all the beautiful things which adorn the Palace of Quiet, and thereby come to a deep insight into the mysteries of Jesus, and into the life of the Church in Christ, and into his very own life in the Church and in Christ. But he is not satisfied with this. His ambition, like that of every true mystic, grows at last until it knows no bounds. Of all things, two in particular he longs to find out.

First, he would like to be shown in what manner he himself is in God.

He has already met with the loving God in the sanctuary of his own soul and contemplated Him there; now what he wishes to see is his own individual self in God.

He does not know whether such a favour can be granted to mortal man or how; but he feels inwardly urged to sigh after it and humbly begs for it. He is aware that in so doing he is only yielding to a pressure coming from within him, though not from himself, but—as he is intimately convinced—from the Holy Spirit.

And then, the second vehement desire, which is growing and ripening in his heart of hearts, is so sublime, so absolutely supreme, that he hardly dares to put it, even to himself, into words. It is to see God in Himself, in His very Self, in His Divine Essence—if this could be granted him here below, in howsoever small a

THE BURNING BUSH

measure—or else he feels he will die of longing and sorrow.

Now, these holy desires please God so much that He vouchsafes to grant them some fulfilment.

One day Fidelis—for such was the name now given him from above—was reading some verses of Exodus, as illustrated on the mosaic pavement of the Palace. He began to ponder deeply over the words which God spoke to Moses from the midst of the burning bush: *I am who am* (Exod. iii, 14). Suddenly a wonderful thing happened.

The Palace of Quiet—pavement, walls, columns, fountain and all—vanished. There he stood on the naked earth and in front of him rose a huge pyramid of gold, or of fire, or of some unknown material, incandescent, piercing the sky. Its brightness was such that nothing already known to him could give an idea of it. And he felt that this was no inanimate object, but living, intensely living, nay, Life itself—essential, superessential, supersubstantial life—the very headspring of all life, the only true life, in one word, God, the Most

THE GOLDEN PYRAMID

Holy Trinity, expressing Himself under this symbolical appearance, to the eyes of his intellect even more than to those of his senses.

To throw himself prostrate on the ground was the work of an instant; but though our Knight hid his face in the dust before the tremendous Majesty of God thus revealed, he did not cease a single instant to see the vision.

It was a perfect pyramid, self-contained, and self-sustaining, for it did not rest on the ground. And it had no aperture of any kind in the shape of either door or window. And from it floated (how shall I describe this?), as it were, a stream of harmonious sound inexpressibly sweet, and a cloud of perfume so exquisite that it did not seem a man could breathe it for any length of time and live. *Sound, perfume,* did I say? But these are coarse figures, though the best at command, to give an idea of what was an absolutely spiritual, nay, a Divine phenomenon.

The whole Palace of Quiet had melted away, it would seem, and our Knight was alone, all alone, with God alone, but instead of terror, this filled him with the deepest feeling of joy he had ever experienced in his life.

There he was, grovelling on the ground, telling God his adoration in inarticulate speech, broken by sighs. There he was in presence of the Infinite Majesty—alone, wretched, void of merits, and yet beloved! Oh the Divine irony of the situation!

And yet he realized that this was as it should be. He felt it was right that these two extremes should meet. He exclaimed between sobs: "My God, my dearly loved God, Most Holy Trinity, such as I am, wretched as I am beyond all words, I long to be united to Thee as Thou art, O Infinite Goodness; that the flames of Thine Infinite Sanctity may consume the rust of my sins and vices. Oh that I may at last be one with Thee in perfect love for ever!"

CHAPTER XXXIII

THE SUPREMEST EXPERIENCE

SUMMARY.—The living Crucifix. Through Him into the Golden Pyramid. What then? How long? Limitations of the transforming Union. Feelings of the Soul about it. Back into the Palace of Quiet. The soul enlarged and what it sighs for. Last days of St. Thomas Aquinas. Knight Fidelis will die of his wound.

AS he concluded this prayer our Knight scrambled to his knees, and fastening his gaze in an ecstasy of adoration upon the bright vision, he stretched out his arms in the form of a cross, and lo and behold, he had no sooner unconsciously struck this attitude, than he descried in front of him at the foot of the Pyramid, a cross, a wooden cross, with its burden of suffering, agonizing humanity.

The representation of the Lamb of God, bleeding away His sacred life, was so vivid, so pathetic, so irresistibly attractive, that he could not repress the impulse: he dragged himself on his knees close to the cross, embraced the feet of his Saviour,

THE BURNING BUSH

bathing them with tears of love and sorrow, then, plucking courage, he arose and cast himself upon the breast of Our Lord, and embracing Him in a transport of love, he strained Him with incredible fervour to his heart, which he felt as though ready to break.

But oh! what was this new marvellous impression?

Whilst thus embracing his crucified Saviour, our Knight felt as though he were passing wholly into Him, nay, through Him and beyond Him and into the very interior of the Golden Pyramid.

It had not been opened to let him in, nor had it closed behind him, and now he felt he was simply engulfed in its infinite depths.

There he was, in the pure, naked, simple Divine Essence, separated from every created thing, dazzled by the infinite splendour, speechless, imageless, motionless as one dead. And, indeed, dead he was to all the world outside, though, in himself, or rather in God, more quick and alert and loving than he had ever been before.

But what did he see in that sanctuary

THE SUPREMEST EXPERIENCE

which the blessed Tri-une God is to Himself? in the primordial, transcending, infinitely pure Divine Essence?

He saw and he saw not. He saw Nothing and he saw All things. He was seized upon and he gave himself up utterly. He saw himself in God as a tiny spark of the same fire as the pyramid itself. One word was spoken to him, only one word, uttered in the midst of an ineffable silence. He himself, in reply, said one word, only one word, not as coming from himself, though his whole self passed into it; one word, not out of the human vocabulary. It was given him; he received it rapturously and hastened to give it back to the Giver: *arcanum verbum*, too sacred to be repeated.

How long did this ecstasy last?

Ah! Who can tell? A passing moment or a century? Was he rapt only in the spirit or also in the flesh? *Nescio, Deus scit: God alone knows* (2 Cor. xii, 2). It was certainly as near an approach as possible on earth to the bliss of eternity which theologians describe, after Boethius, as "the full and perfect possession, all at once, of a limitless life: *Interminabilis vitae tota simul et perfecta possessio*" (*De Consol. Philos.*, Tit. iii, Pr. 2).

There are no successive moments in such a duration: all is given in an immutable Now. God is to Hmself His eternity, His own duration, absolutely changeless. Now, it seems that something of this immutability of God enters into the contemplative during such moments of ecstasy, almost as though he were turned into God.

Of course, we must not fall into the error of pantheists: we must admit that this sort of Divine visitation with which some devout persons have been sometimes favoured is, of its nature, purely accidental. It in no way affronts the inviolable Divine Essence, nor, either, does it alter the fundamental limitations of the man rapt in God. A created thing can never become the Uncreated, nor could a secondary cause become one essentially with the *Causa Prima*. The finite spirit for ever remains within its own finite boundaries, nor would he be content, if—by supposition of an impossible thing—it were offered to him to become anything but what it is. In this firm, humble attitude, he renders to God a noble tribute of adora-

THE SUPREMEST EXPERIENCE

tion. It is as though he protested: *Loquar ad Dominum meum cum sim pulvis et cinis.* Indeed, *I am but dust and ashes, but let me say this:* Thou my God, art the only Holy, the only Lord, the only Most High: *Tu solus Sanctus, tu solus Dominus, tu solus Altissimus!*

When he came to himself again, Knight Fidelis found himself once more in the Palace of Quiet. But although every object in that palace had, from the fact of his recent experience, put on, so to speak, a fresh meaning, at once deeper and more delightful, nevertheless he found it difficult, nay painful, extremely painful, to re-adjust himself to it.

Long ago, quite at the beginning of his sojourn in that blessed, enchanted abode, it had seemed to him that for the remainder of his life (were it even to be prolonged to the years of Mathusala), never would he tire of the holy delight of the Palace of Quiet: but what he then judged impossible is now happening to him. More than ever does he enjoy its delights; he penetrates into the meaning of every single detail of its wondrous architecture and ornamentation, and they stir him as never before; but somehow himself is changed.

Through burning contact with the Divine Essence, his soul has become so enlarged that nothing on earth will any longer be capable of filling and satiating it, not even the full banquet of religion as the Catholic Church spreads it before the children of Divine grace. The soul that has gone through the supremest mystical experience craves for more than this. Yes, for more than faith and hope. Even for more than charity as it is to be had here below; for more than the precious life-giving Sacraments; more than the veiled presence of her Beloved in His Holy Eucharist; more than the actual communion of His living flesh and blood; more than the enjoyment of the perpetual presence within her of the Holy Ghost, with all His gifts and fruits and beatitudes. My God! even more than all these? What then? What?

Oh! nothing less than the vision of God, face to face.

Nothing short of this will now satiate the hunger of that man, the sublime ambi-

THE SUPREMEST EXPERIENCE

tion of his soul, aroused to its highest pitch.

He has lost all interest in what goes on around him; lost interest in his former occupations, in his dearest works. Thus, St. Thomas Aquinas, in the last days of his life, when urged by his faithful amanuensis to add something to his unfinished *Summa Theologica*, would reply: "Oh! I can no more. Brother Reginald, all this looks to me now as mere chaff."

So Knight Fidelis drags himself along, sighing incessantly. The daintiest food of Christian piety which he used to relish so much, the Divine Scriptures, the lives and writings of the dear Saints, the flesh and blood of his Saviour, offered upon the altar and received in Holy Communion, do but exasperate his hunger and heighten the fever that is consuming him. He is languishing for heaven, fainting away; sorely smitten with the golden arrow tipped with flame from the altar of God. Oh! he will die, he will surely and swiftly die of his wound.

Blessed death! May mine own be like unto this!

EPILOGUE

I ASK again: "My soul, what have we done?

"Can it be that we set out to attempt this impossible task of declaring God?"

God!

A short word. Three letters and that is all. One syllable. A breath!

But the Thing, ah! the Thing it means; the One, the Tri-une, *He that is*, and nothing else is in comparison; have we succeeded in bringing Him to view before the mind's eye?

We wished to. Have we succeeded?

No! no! A thousand times no! It were too egregious a delusion to believe it. Indeed, how could we expect to succeed in this rash enterprise—especially we, we of all men?

The last four chapters of the Book of Job contain a Divine rebuke to that holy man for his failure to speak of God and His works worthily. A few short extracts will here serve our purpose:

EPILOGUE

Then the Lord answered Job out of a whirlwind and said:

Who is this that wrappeth up sentences in unskilled words?

Gird up thy loins like a man. I will ask thee, and answer thou Me.

Where wast thou when I laid the foundations of the earth? Tell Me if thou hast understanding.

Who hath laid the measure thereof, if thou knowest? Or who hath stretched the line upon it?

Upon what are its bases grounded? Or who laid the corner-stone thereof,

When the morning stars praised Me together, and all the sons of God made a joyful melody?

Didst thou know then that thou shouldst be born? And didst thou know the number of thy days?

Hast thou entered into the storehouses of the snow? Or hast thou beheld the treasures of the hail?

Shalt thou be able to join together the shining stars the Pleiades, or canst thou stop the turning about of Arcturus?

Canst thou bring forth the day star in its

time, and make the evening star to rise upon the children of the earth?

Dost thou know the order of heaven? And canst thou set down the reason thereof on the earth?

Job xxxviii, *passim.*

Then Job answered the Lord, and said: What can I answer, who have spoken inconsiderately? I will lay my hand upon my mouth.

One thing I have spoken, which I wish I had not said: and another, to which I will add no more.

Job xxxix, 33-35.

And I also, in my turn, will answer the Lord and say with a deep sense of my utter failure and asking pardon for my rashness: *One thing I have spoken,* in the first part of this treatise—namely, the mystery of the Most Holy Trinity—*which I almost wish I had not said. And another*—in the second and third parts, about the works of God and His wonderful dealings with a fervent soul—*to which I will add no more.*

THE END

Printed in the United States
1209500001B/250